Mastering Simplicity

A LIFE IN THE KITCHEN

Mastering Simplicity

A LIFE IN THE KITCHEN

Christian Delouvrier

JENNIFER LEUZZI

PHOTOGRAPHS BY MICHEL ARNAUD

JOHN WILEY & SONS, INC.

For general information on our other products and services or for technical support, please contact our Customer Care Department within the United States at (800) 762-2974, outside the United States at (317) 572-3993 or fax (317) 572-4002.

Wiley also publishes its books in a variety of electronic formats. Some content that appears in print may not be available in electronic books. For more information about Wiley products, visit our web site at www.wiley.com.

LIBRARY OF CONGRESS CATALOGING-IN-PUBLICATION DATA

Delouvrier, Christian.
 Mastering simplicity : a life in the kitchen / Christian Delouvrier and Jennifer Leuzzi.
    p. cm.
Includes index.
 ISBN 0-471-41359-3 (Cloth)
 1. Cookery, French. I. Leuzzi, Jennifer. II. Title.
TX719.D373412 2003
641.5944--dc21
                               2003007456

Designed by Vertigo Design, NYC
www.vertigodesignnyc.com

Printed in the United States of America

10 9 8 7 6 5 4 3 2 1

WITH DEEPEST LOVE,
this book is dedicated to my mother and to
my grandmothers, Marie Louise and Mamoune,
who taught me that food must nourish the soul
as well as the body

Contents

Acknowledgments

This book would not have been written without so many wonderful people in my life, both in and out of the kitchen.

First and most important, my wife, Mary, and my children, Marc and Christine, who have allowed me to immerse myself in the kitchen and remained uncomplaining throughout long hours away from home and missed holidays and family celebrations. My love for them is boundless.

My soeur, Lynette, who is the link between my life in America and my French roots.

My American family, the Dunns, especially Grandpa John Dunn whose wisdom and guidance provide the cornerstone that supports the resilient spirit of the Dunn clan.

All of the cuisiniers from whom I have learned and who have shown me that passion is the magic ingredient in any dish, specifically Georges Buffeteau, Patrice Caillot, Francis Hinault, Charles Lejay, Michel Martin, and Alain Senderens.

Members of my brigades:

From the past—Jonathan Beno, Chris Broberg, Ed Brown, Michael Colameco, and his wife, Hayjung, John Di Leo, Luc Dimnet, Karen Dupont, Xavier Grenet, Eric le Belge, Philip Longobardi, Eric Martin, Laurent Poupard, Andre Renard, Ed Stone, Christophe Toury, and Bob Weiner.

In the present—Robert Bagli, Bill Brasil, Corey Colton, Juan Cuevas, Yuhi Fujinaga, Franck, Geret, Robert Goodhue, Adam Greenberg, Huyuh Hung, Tomo Kobayashi, Craig Koketsu, Cory Lee, Shane McBride, Margaret McMahon, Sergiio Mendez, Emilio Mendoza, Aki Moroto, Matt Murphy, Joe Perrone, Michael Stanton, Justin Toth, Vinny Troiano, Jose Vargas, German Vasquez, James Wagner, Damon Wise.

I am particularly indebted to Craig, Juan, Shane, and Vinny for their daily dose of inspiration and strength, especially on the days when the weather is rough!

The managing staff of the hotels in my past, most specifically Reinhart Neubert, Dimitri Zarikos, and Wolf Walther.

The great staff of Lespinasse and the St. Regis Hotel, in particular, Gunther Richter and Atef Mankarios form the management team and Jean Phillipe Leloup and Danielle Nally in the dining room.

The purveyors who provide me with the best that I can ask for: Bernardaud, Gerard Boyer, Braggard and Spitler, The Chef Garden, D'Artagnan, Gourmand, Hudson Valley Foie Gras, Ideal Cheese, Indian Rock, La Reserve Seafood, Dominique Mille of Paterno, Rod Mitchell, Mushrooms and More, Piccinini Brothers, Pierless, Plantin America, J.P. Prince, M. Slavin and Sons, Jacques Torres Chocolate, Yama Seafood

Rudy Vaccari for his friendship through the years

Jean-Louis Dumonet for the passion we share

In fond remembrance of Jean Louis Palladin

My deepest gratitude goes to the team that helped me transform my thoughts to the written word:

A heartfelt thank you to my agent, Mickey Choate of The Lescher Agency, who saw a book long before I ever thought of one and who knows my cooking better than I do. His belief in me was unwavering and his help and support became my buoy in strong seas.

Jennifer Leuzzi, who did all of the groundwork and led me in the right direction.

Michel Arnaud—what can I say about two Frenchmen in the kitchen? Your photographs capture the essence of my cooking.

Alison Lew and Renata De Oliveira of Vertigo Design, NYC—your design and art direction skills brought my words to life in my vision.

Pamela Chirls, my editor at Wiley: your interest was the spark that ignited the fire.

Judith Choate, who listened to my stories, made my words come alive on the page, and gave me the book that I dreamed about.

If I have missed anyone it is not with intent—I deeply appreciate the help and guidance that you have generously shown me throughout my career.

—*Christian Delourier*

I would like to thank Christian for the opportunity to write this book with him, Mickey for making it a reality, Judie and Steve for sharing their wisdom, Lawrence and Patricia for Paris, and Laurent for his endless inspiration.

—*Jennifer Leuzzi*

Mastering Simplicity

A LIFE IN THE KITCHEN

The way I cook

When I began to think about collecting my recipes into a book, I wondered how I could find the words to talk about something that had been my obsession for so long. I knew that I could cook almost anything but I had no idea how to translate my passion onto paper. Besides, I still often think in French, which further complicated decoding my thoughts. As I began to focus on the problem, I realized that before I could write about how I came to cook I would have to think about the hows and whys of the way I cook. All of this led me to think about my French heritage and the traditions upon which my career in the kitchen has been built.

It is extremely difficult not to sound chauvinistic when talking about the cuisine of your native land and it is particularly difficult when you are French. But you have to admit that, without dispute, French cuisine is the world's most important with its influence impacting almost all others, especially in the arena of fine dining. In part, this is because from the earliest moment in life, we French are focused on what the day will bring to the table. We think and talk about the foods we will eat, we shop in earnest for the freshest local ingredients, we cook with respect, and we consume our meals in relaxed pleasure. In a word, we love to cook and we love to eat!

I believe that my style of cooking has been formed by this intense culinary tradition that is so typically French. Not only is it found in the commercial kitchen but it is also firmly based in the home kitchen as well as at the table. As I have experienced the cuisines of the world, I have found that there is almost no other where freshness, respect for the natural flavors of the raw ingredients, locality, seasonality, and the almost indefinable *terroir* so vitally impact on the meals brought to the table.

In fact, I have begun to think that the love of all things culinary has gone beyond tradition and heritage and is now imprinted on the human root stock of France.

Although France has fourteen distinct regions, each with its own local fare, each region spills over its perimeters to create a national cuisine. In school, we often referred to our country as *l'Hexagone* because of its six-sided shape; it is these many borders that open the country to diffuse climates and the bounty of natural resources and products. The cuisine of France is so intrinsically varied that it covers almost every style and preparation. It is primarily the natural resources—the sea, the land, the water, the weather . . . in short, the *terroir*—that combine to bring together all of the regional specialties that create a national table.

Throughout France, each region has products and dishes that mean authentic French cooking to the locals, and even though they may be served in other parts of the country (or the world) they are never so delicious as when eaten "at home." At opposite sides, the Atlantic Ocean and the Mediterranean Sea offer deeply differing climates and a bounty of widely extreme foods. In the north, where the Atlantic hits the shores of Normandy and Brittany, oysters, langoustines, lobsters, scallops, prawns, crayfish, and an endless variety of other fish and seafood, as well as apples, rich milk, cream and cheeses, lamb, and hearty sausages are found. Nationally prescribed dishes such as *tripes à la mode de Caen and crêpes* also find their home in this cool, pastoral climate. On the other horizon, we have olives and olive oil, garlic, herbs, tomatoes, anchovies, truffles, and marvelous fruits and vegetables nourished by the hot southern sun. The warm seas offer copious fish, some of which are the base for the truly national fish stews of *bouillabaisse* (see page 125) and *bourride*. All of the other regions have defining foods that combine to spell traditional French cooking all over the world.

Along with the foods of France, its wines and liqueurs give balance to the traditional table. In fact, I cannot remember ever having a meal without wine in my parents' home. Specific wine-producing regions provide a great many of the world's most treasured vintages while the beers and ciders of the countryside are the perfect accompaniment to the rich dishes of Alsace-Lorraine and Brittany. Even nonalcoholic drinks such as *citron pressé* zing with pure and natural flavors for those who do not choose to imbibe spirits. And, of course, no table is set without a bottle or two of one of France's famous mineral waters to aid in digestion. I would say that, in France, no meal is considered complete without a bottle of wine to toast the cook and some mineral water to calm the liver!

I am always amused to note that when people think of French cooking they only think of fancy restaurants and rich sauces. These are, of course, a defining part of French cooking, but they are not the only part. Many of the traditions that I honor and the techniques that I follow were established by French housewives such as my mother and grandmothers. The best food in France is not, contrary to popular opinion, found in those restaurants featured in the pages of the *Guide Michelin*. Most often the best food is eaten in homes, with family and friends around the table, where women are the undisputed four-star chefs. While the great professional chefs are usually men, women cooks have frequently been their inspiration. For generations, women have passed on family recipes and the pride that comes from good food prepared well and served for the pleasure of others. This sentiment is really the basis for the French culinary tradition and for my own method in the kitchen.

I still use many of the classic techniques that I learned as an apprentice and young cook and, as I worked on this book, I realized that my cooking philosophy and style had not really changed very much throughout the many years that I have spent working to perfect my craft. Of course, as I discovered new products and once-exotic ingredients became readily available, I incorporated them into my cooking but the basic principles remained the same over the years. Whether braising, making stocks or *confit*, roasting or sautéeing, great cooking begins with a search for the finest ingredients, just as it did when I was a boy. This is followed by an appreciation of and respect for their natural flavors. Finally, a love of food is necessary to develop a discerning palate. Over the years, as my cooking environments changed, these simple, classically taught guidelines remained the same.

As I worked on this book, I realized that I have, in recent years, altered some of my cooking techniques slightly because I learned more about the raw ingredients themselves. For instance, other than when braising, I now cook everything for far shorter periods than I once did. Vegetables were once cooked until very soft, often covered with heavy sauces and seasonings, with many of the nutrients cooked out. I now know that they not only taste better but are better for you when cooked lightly until just tender (and not, as is often done, with crunch and rawness still evident) with minimal saucing and seasoning. The purity of flavor and the perfection of texture are the reigning ideals on the plate.

In the restaurant kitchen and at home, most cooks are using far more olive (and other fruit and vegetable) oil than butter for health reasons and to highlight the freshness of flavor. Fish is often seared quickly, skin side down, seasoned lightly with salt and pepper, and finished in a hot oven to retain its moisture and delicate flavor. In short, I (and most other cooks) am cooking more to protect the integrity of the product than to showcase the artistry of the chef.

To do this, I strongly believe that a good cook needs a strong foundation of basic skills and techniques as well as a fine-tuning of the senses. For me, this was realized though the ancient French apprentice system that began in childhood and has, even in France, almost faded from the educational system. In France as in America, fine culinary schools and superbly trained chefs now carry on this tradition. Culinary techniques can be easily taught and skill can be accomplished through practice, but taste must be developed over many, many years through continual use and lots of trial and error. It also helps to come from a culture (and a family) that values a culinary tradition and has a respect for its agricultural heritage. I have come to realize that once I absorbed the classic techniques and became fairly adept at them and developed my senses to instinctively know what flavors, techniques, and products would work together, it has become increasingly easy to take my kitchen and my guests in the dining room on a culinary adventure.

The first rule of cooking well is that the primary ingredients become the building blocks of any dish. I always begin with a respect for the texture and taste of each ingredient that I am considering. I aim to enhance and showcase the individual flavor of each ingredient, not to hide it. To me, this means that I must find balance in any dish that I create. Balance comes from understanding the role each ingredient plays in a specific recipe.

Finding the balance of a dish might be as complicated as the three stages required to cook the perfectly poached chicken (see page 34) whereby each stage has the opportunity to add its particular flavor to the final dish. In the first stage, onions, cut in half with their peel still intact, are caramelized and then cooked with raw chicken and tomato to make the initial broth. This strained broth from the first stage is then cooked with fresh tomato, leeks, and carrots to build up the bouillon. In the final stage, a blanched chicken is cooked in the strained stage-two bouillon. This reinforced broth is further infused with the mellowness of one raw carrot and one leek. Through the stages the acidic tomato adds layers of sweet and sour, clarifies the bouillon, and adds a gentle and unexpected nuance of perfumed acidity. On the simpler side, balance may also be achieved when a perfectly ripe, just-picked tomato is served at garden temperature with a sprinkle of sea salt to draw out and accent its naturally sweet, slightly biting flavor.

Indispensable to the way I cook is the ancient technique of nourishment. To nourish a dish, I take something, usually meat, that is lean and is prone to dryness when cooked, and introduce fat into it. This might mean something as simple as a long slow braise in a rich liquid as is often done to lean, tough meats, or something as unexpected as wrapping a piece of cod or monkfish with blanched (to draw out the excess salinity) bacon, or as complex as "nourishing" a poached chicken bouillon to a luxurious creaminess with deliciously fragrant and sensual foie gras (see page 260).

The fat from the foie gras will nourish both the bouillon and the meat of the chicken to add an almost indefinable elegance to what is otherwise a very simple dish.

One of the most lasting lessons that I learned as a young cook came from the brilliant chef, Alain Senderens. He held a tomato in his hands and said, "Look at this beautiful tomato and think about what it took to make it grow. There was the earth, the sun, plenty of water, and the gardener who tended it. This is a gift that comes to you. You don't have the right to mistreat it." I believe that it is from this very basic but essential respect for the land and its bounty that the conscience of the chef is born. It is imperative that we improve on what nature has provided. If I can't make it better than it was when it was harvested, then I leave it alone. This rule is at the very foundation of how I cook.

When giving the ingredients the respect due them, I believe that it is necessary to eliminate waste. I have found this kitchen rule to be true no matter the cuisine. I have seen Chinese cooks, just like the French, use the entire chicken, including the feet and the beak. Many vegetables offer their greens as well as their root to the inventive cook. Scraps and bits and pieces can be combined to create soups, broths, and stews. This efficiency and economy commands the ingenuity of the cook but it also creates a harmony at the table because the dish will contain a repetition of flavors in a reflective layering.

Every recipe is like a map. It will direct you to go from A to B to C to get to D. It may also serve as a guideline to other recipes. The technique that it highlights may also be applied to many other recipes. Usually it is the main ingredient that is the "star" with the vegetables, sauces, and seasonings the "supporting cast." Sometimes it is the "supporting cast" that takes center stage. It is the personal interpretation of the recipe that is the deciding factor for the intent of the dish as I believe that any recipe is simply the literal translation of the personality of the cook. In the restaurant, it is my way of giving a bit of myself to our guests—a bit of my life experiences as a cook and as a human being. And, at home, it is the cook's gift to family and friends.

Beyond the systematic rules of a recipe, cooking will often take you on an adventure. With many of my recipes, especially those from my youth, I am transported back to a France that is slowly fading from view. Some recipes, through their ingredients and techniques, transport me to many different places throughout the world, some that I've actually visited and others that I know only through the cuisine. For me, thinking about cooking and translating my recipes to the written word have been quite like creating an internal Discovery Channel. I hope that I will take you along on my trip.

As I read through my recipes and recollections I find that my book has become so much more than a cookbook. Writing it caused me to think about my life in the kitchen; it enriched me and made me more aware of the world around me. It is really a culinary memoir that relates my life with food, professionally and on a deeply personal level. It can be read from beginning to end like a storybook or bit by bit, recipe by recipe. My hope for you, the reader and the cook, is that while you use this book you will learn not only the way I cook but also how I came to cook the way that I do, and that once you learn this, you will be able to take these lessons to your own kitchen and improvise your own recipes in the classic French manner. Bon Appétit!

Hows and Whys

During forty years of cooking, I have developed some basic rules and habits that I always follow. Some are driven by personal taste, some by practicality, some through the evolution of culinary knowledge, and others by tradition. I cannot reiterate often enough (as I do daily in the kitchen) that all good cooking begins with the quality and integrity of the raw ingredients. Therefore, it starts not in the kitchen but first in its origin and then in the supermarket, farmer's market, butcher shop, fishmonger, or wherever the ingredient is purchased—or, if you are very lucky, in your own garden or farmyard where you pick and choose as needed. It is very easy to remember that the better the beginning product, the better the end result.

If you are shopping with a particular recipe in mind and the ingredients for it do not look especially inviting, rethink your menu or revise the recipe. For instance, if an apple tart is on the menu and apples don't seem prime, replace them with pears or plums or whatever fruit is at its peak. It is far more important that the dish be as flavorful as it can be than it is to follow a recipe to the letter. The desire of the chef to serve something beautifully fresh and fairly priced from the day's market is one of the reasons why so many restaurants feature a *plat du jour* (special of the day). This is a good rule to follow at home as well.

I always use products as they come into season so that I can showcase their finest flavor. I do understand how alluring a bunch of bright green asparagus can be under a gray, winter sky but I can guarantee that it will never live up to the memory of spring's first stalks. Of course, I only use fresh ingredients, never frozen or canned, and preferably those that are organically grown or naturally raised from local farmers whom I know and trust. Luckily, as a chef in New York City, I do have the advantage of working directly with producers to have them grow or raise products exactly to my specifications. However, there are now so many farmer's markets and specialty food stores across the country that most cooks have the opportunity to purchase very fresh, natural ingredients in season.

My basic techniques are no different from those taught to all beginning cooks, and most of them are recognizable to any knowledgeable home cook. However, for a few of the techniques that I use frequently, it is necessary to understand why they are so integral to my style of cooking.

In almost every case, I blanch vegetables and cured meats so that they retain their integrity when assimilated into a dish. For cured meats, blanching removes the excess salt and for fresh meat it eliminates the raw taste and begins the tenderizing process. For vegetables, I blanch to set the color. When blanching green vegetables and fresh meats, I use salted water. For other vegetables and cured meats, I use unsalted water. Vegetables are always placed in rapidly boiling water for a very brief period (about 30 seconds) and immediately drained and placed in an ice-water bath or under very cold running water to stop the cooking process. In kitchen talk, this technique is referred to as "shocking." Meats, either fresh or cured, are placed in cold water over high heat and brought to a boil. Once boiling, they are immediately removed from the water, thoroughly drained, and then immediately "shocked" in an ice-water bath. Never leave the "shocked" ingredient in the ice-water bath or under cold running water for an extended period, as this will only serve to drain off flavor and create excess water in it; "shock" just long enough to stop the cooking process.

I have noticed that a term professional chefs have used forever, "to sweat," has recently come into common usage. It is a cooking technique that I use often and it is important that it be completely understood. It is most frequently used to begin the cooking process for aromatics (onions, shallots, garlic). When it is necessary to soften an ingredient without adding color to it, it is cooked very slowly in some type of fat just long enough to remove the raw taste, soften the texture, and release and blend the flavors without browning or coloring. Once aromatics are browned or colored, the sugars have been released and they have begun to caramelize, which will add a very different flavor to the finished dish. In my dishes, it is usually the basic flavor I am seeking, not the sugary impact of caramelization.

One of the classic techniques that I still use with great frequency is long periods of marinating. Once, extended marinades were primarily used to cover the fact that the meat (often game) had spoiled and, without the addition of the acidic marinade and pungent seasonings, was quite inedible. Through culinary evolution, marinades (usually comprised of aromatics, seasoning vegetables, herbs and/or spices, and some type of acid such as wine, vinegar, citrus juices, or cider) have come to be used to tenderize wild game and tough or lean cuts of farm-raised meat. The acid in the marinade is essential to break down the tough fibers and muscle in the meat and the seasonings create mellow flavor. I use complex marinades for many classic and family dishes for which braising will be the cooking method. Because braising is a very long, slow cooking process done through wet heat in a tightly covered pot over extremely low heat, periods of extended marination help infuse deep, rich flavor into the meat as well as into the sauce. For some dishes such as Coq au Vin (see page 38), the dish will have an extended period of marination as well as be cooked in a sauce based on the marinade. This insures that the final flavor of the dish is intense, multi-layered, and complex. This sounds complicated, I know, but it really is quite simple. It only takes time and patience.

One of the most ancient of all classic cooking techniques is *confit*. Traditionally, meat (usually pork, duck, or goose) was salted and cooked for a very long period in its own fat. The meat, which was rendered meltingly tender by the cooking process, was then packed into a crock and covered with the cooking fat that would seal and preserve it. In my grandmother's day, this method was used primarily for practical reasons because there was no refrigeration, but meat cured in this manner is so delicious that the method is still practiced today although, I must admit, infrequently in the home kitchen. It is so much a part of my culinary heritage that I continue to search for ways to incorporate confit into contemporary dishes. For instance, in my Confit of Baby Pig (see page 266) I use the technique not as a preservative but to impart a sublime texture to the succulent meat. I confit the baby pig because long, slow cooking in fat nourishes the very lean meat and highlights the extremely subtle flavor. I cook it in duck fat to richly season and mellow the flavor, because if I used pork fat the final taste would be too fatty and "porky" on the palate and would consequently overpower the delicate meat.

In my more recent recipes, the layering of flavors has become vitally important to my style of cooking. Although on the final plate the presentation might seem intricate and demanding, it really is simply the sum of many parts, with each one able to stand on its own. Sometimes the layering is accomplished by cooking one main ingredient in differing styles. For instance, I might start a duck breast by cooking the whole duck on the rotisserie; then I bone out the breast and poach it in a very aromatic stock that complements the rich duck; and finally I would finish cooking the breast in a very hot oven to sear the skin. All of the cooking times will be short so that the meat is not overcooked and dry, but each cooking method will impart its own particular flavor to the final, quite indefinable, taste.

I particularly like to layer flavor with a couple of different styles of one type of meat (along with the appropriate accompaniments) on the finished plate. To begin the layering, I might use a braised dish in which I have used the long, slow braise to hide the shortcomings (such as too little meat) of beef ribs and to highlight their intense meaty flavor; then, I might layer some slices of sirloin (say, a shell steak), using the rare, juicy and slightly chewy meat to complement the tenderness and deep beefiness of the braise. I would, in this instance, use shell steak rather than filet mignon because it is not quite as lean and is, therefore, much tastier and packs more punch on the plate.

The hows and whys of the way I cook are quite simple but they are, for the most part, time-consuming. In the restaurant kitchen, I have a brigade of cooks and a staff of helpers to assure that I can reach for perfection every day. I realize that this is difficult to do at home, but if you plan in advance and allow plenty of time, you too can create complex dishes with ease.

Family Cooking
Boulogne-Sur-Gesse, France

Although I have been cooking almost my entire life, very few people ask why I decided to become a chef. And, frankly, it wasn't until I started working on this book that I gave any thought to the reasons for my choice of a career in the kitchen. When I first thought about becoming a chef, I thought that it was because I didn't have any particular intellectual interest to pursue, but I now know that it was the food and cooks of my childhood that made me want to be a chef. It was the aromas wafting from the kitchen and the warmth of the dining room that planted the seeds for a culinary path. Somehow, subliminally, I wanted to recreate this sense of well-being in my adult life.

I was born in 1945 in the small town of Boulogne-sur-Gesse in the southwestern region of France known as Gascony. We were a tight-knit family with my grandparents very much a part of my daily life. On alternating Sundays we would take our meal with one set of grandparents, one Sunday in the countryside and the next in Toulouse. You could almost eat the air as you walked into either house, as it was so dense with the fragrant smell of the *daube* (see page 50) or the *poule au pot* (see page 34) and the sugary scent of the *riz au lait* (see page 60) or the *tarte aux pommes* (see page 56). My grandmothers, with their careful brewing of rich, intense braised meals, gave me my first knowledge of a good *saucier* and, from that, a love of deeply flavored sauces.

My father's family had a long history in the food business. His grandparents had a dairy farm called *L'Herbette* which his father eventually ran, buying and selling cows and their milk and working with restaurants in the area. His mother, Marie Louise, whom I called Manoune, was an extraordinary cook who, while her husband tended his cows, ran a small *pension de famille* at the house. She cooked the

meals and kept up the boarders' rooms. Those passing through would also stop to take their meals in Marie Louise's dining room. Business was so good that, by 1918, my grandparents expanded by opening Café Delouvrier in Montpellier. Manoune cooked at the café and also continued to run the pension at home. However, in 1925 they sold the farm and put all of their energy into running the very successful café.

My grandparents eventually moved to Montpellier and continued to run cafés for the remainder of their life together. When my grandfather passed away, Manoune returned to running a pension de famille for many years and finally opened another small country restaurant. One of my first restaurant memories is with Manoune when I was six or seven. She took me to a small café in her hometown where I ate a nettle soup (see page 22) that was so unforgettably delicious that I still serve a version of it today at Lespinasse.

I also still remember the way Manoune used to set the table—old china with delicate pastel flowers, rustic glasses, immense silver knives with ivory handles—such care was centered on her family and the food that she would be serving. I think that Manoune's influence can still be seen in my own approach to cooking and to the table.

My mother's parents also had a farm where I could run free and experience rural life. I remember a day—perhaps I was four or so—chasing the chickens, ducks, and geese around the yard when two or three nasty geese, wings spread and necks thrust forth like swords, had enough of my foolishness and chased me right into a patch of stinging nettles. I think that this was my first visceral encounter with those wonderful products of Gascogne—geese, ducks, and nettles!

Fricassée de Cèpes Bordelaise
FRICASSEE OF PORCINI MUSHROOMS

La Soupe d'Ortie de Ma Grand-mère
MY GRANDMOTHER'S NETTLE SOUP

Garbure de Légumes, Façon Gasconne
VEGETABLE SOUP IN THE GASCON STYLE

Choux-fleur Suzanne
SUZANNE'S CAULIFLOWER

Artichauts Barigoules
ARTICHOKES WITH WHITE WINE AND HERBS

Fagot d'Ecrevisses des Ruisseaux de l'Aveyron
BOILED CRAYFISH

La Poule au Pot et Sa Garniture de Choux, Carrotes, et
Son Farci à la Cansalade
CHICKEN IN A POT WITH STUFFING AND VEGETABLES

Bouillon de Poule aux Vermicelles
CHICKEN BOUILLON WITH NOODLES

Coq au Vin
BRAISED CHICKEN IN RED WINE

Cassoulet
CASSOULET

Boeuf en Daube
GASCON BEEF STEW

Carré de Porc aux Pruneaux, Endives Braisées
ROAST PORK LOIN WITH PRUNES AND BRAISED ENDIVES

Tarte aux Pommes Bonne Maman
MOM'S APPLE TART

Soufflé au Chocolat
DARK CHOCOLATE SOUFFLÉ

Riz au Lait Marie Louise
MARIE LOUISE'S RICE PUDDING

Fricassée de cèpes

bordelaise

● SERVES 4

In the forests of the French Pyrénées Mountains and in Gascony, the season for cèpe mushrooms begins at the end of September and lasts until the end of November. During this period, we would often go for family walks in the woods just on the edge of town to hunt for the earthy, meaty cèpes. Usually it was my mother, her parents, our cousin Louis, and of course, me. My grandmother and Louis both knew which were the good mushrooms and which were poisonous. I don't know how they learned this; it seemed to be something they just knew. We were fortunate for their knowledge because there is a poisonous mushroom called a bolet de satan that looks exactly like a cèpe. Often I would pick one of these by accident and then Louis would say "non, ce n'est pas bon ça, mon petit."

Sometimes I would also go mushroom hunting with my friends for fun on the weekends or after school. When we had gathered enough to fill our baskets, we would quickly take them back home for our mothers to cook. I liked to bring mine to my grandmother because she always cooked them right away even if it was just for me to have as a snack or a light lunch. My mother, on the other hand, liked to preserve them in mason jars with duck fat and a little bit of salt and pepper to eat later in the year, and this was never as satisfying.

8 medium cèpes or porcini mushrooms

3 tablespoons duck fat

2 tablespoons unsalted butter

3 medium shallots, peeled and finely chopped

2 tablespoons finely chopped fresh flat-leaf parsley

3 cloves garlic, peeled and finely chopped

Coarse salt to taste

Coarsely ground black pepper to taste

1 Clean the cèpes of all debris by gently wiping them with a damp cloth or paper towel. Do not wash them under running water, as they will absorb too much water and this will dilute their flavor. Additionally, the excess water will increase the time they take to cook. Using a paring knife, peel the outside skin of the stems and trim them by ¼ inch to remove all of the base dirt. Slice, lengthwise, into ¼-inch-thick pieces.

2 Heat 2 tablespoons of the duck fat in a 12-inch heavy-duty sauté pan over medium heat. Add the cèpes and sauté for 5 minutes or until they have sweat (see page 8) their liquid and are soft, taking great care that they do not brown at all. This sauté removes all of the water from the mushroom to concentrate the intense flavor. Transfer the cèpes to a colander and drain off and discard the liquid. (This mushroom water can also be saved, covered, and refrigerated, for one week or frozen for up to four weeks. Add it to stocks or soups that have mushrooms in the recipe in place of water for additional flavor.)

3 Place the remaining 1 tablespoon of duck fat into the sauté pan over medium-high heat. When the fat begins to smoke, add the cèpes and sauté them for about 3 to 4 minutes or until they are golden brown and crispy. Since all of the excess liquid has been removed in the first sauté, a nice golden crust should form. (If there is excess liquid, remove the pan from the heat and drain off the liquid. Return the pan to medium-high heat and sauté the mushrooms until the crust forms.)

4 Remove the pan from the heat and add the butter, shallots, parsley, and garlic, stirring until the butter is melted. Arrange on a serving platter with a sprinkling of coarse salt and coarsely ground pepper to taste and serve.

SERVING SUGGESTION As cèpes are in season in the fall months, this is an excellent side dish for any roasted meat or poultry that you would normally serve at this time of year. The flavors are so direct that it is easy to match the dish with everything from veal to pork to duck or chicken. Fricassée de Cèpes also makes an appealing appetizer for a more formal dinner.

La soupe d'ortie de

MY GRANDMOTHER'S NETTLE SOUP

ma grand-mère

● SERVES 4

Behind my grandmother's house, between the road and the garden, wild nettles would begin to sprout up each spring. Nettles are really a weed, with long thin leaves that have small sharp hairs along the edges. Nettles grew spontaneously along the edge of the garden, by the side of the road, or against the walls of the yard or house. We would carefully cut or pull off the branches of leaves, chop them up into small pieces, and put them immediately into a pot of water on the stove to make soup. This is a perfect example of my grandmother's cooking, the way she would take things directly from the earth and put them into the pot.

Later on, as I learned a more refined style of cooking, I discovered that, to make them easier to handle, nettles can be blanched ahead of time to soften the prickly edges. After trying this method, I can't recommend it; nettles are so delicate in flavor (as are many green leafy vegetables), blanching removes too much of their flavor.

I have given an optional step of whisking a tablespoon of butter into the soup so as to create a smooth and silky texture that is quite refined and pleasant on the palate. It also adds a little richness, but if you are counting calories, it truly is not necessary.

2 tablespoons duck fat

1 medium onion, peeled and cut into 1-inch dice

1½ pounds fresh nettles

3 ounces fresh sorrel

1 clove garlic, peeled

1 sprig fresh thyme

¼ teaspoon coarse salt plus more to taste

3 cups Bouillon de Poule (see page 282)

1 large Idaho potato, peeled and sliced

Coarse salt to taste

Freshly ground pepper to taste

1 tablespoon unsalted butter, optional

3 tablespoons crème fraîche

1. Heat the duck fat in a 3- to 4-quart heavy-duty Dutch oven over medium heat, add the onion, and cook for 4 to 5 minutes or until the onions have sweat their moisture and are soft, taking care that they do not brown.

2. Add the nettles, sorrel, garlic, and thyme, and continue to cook for about 2 to 3 minutes or until the vegetables have begun to sweat some of their liquid. Add the ¼ teaspoon salt. Cover the pan and continue to cook for 3 minutes to extract the water from the greens. (The liquid from the vegetables will add additional flavor to the soup.)

3. Add the bouillon and bring to a boil. Immediately add the potato and reduce the heat to medium. Simmer for 15 to 20 minutes or until the potato is tender.

4. Carefully pour the hot soup into a blender and process to a smooth puree. You may have to do this in batches.

5. Place the puree into a clean saucepan over medium heat and bring it to a simmer. Taste and adjust the seasoning with salt and pepper.

6. Remove from the heat and, if using, whisk in the tablespoon of butter.

7. If not using the optional butter, immediately whisk in the crème fraîche, and serve very hot.

Garbure de légumes,

façon Gasconne

● SERVES 4

This is a typical French, winter Sunday night supper dish, meant to be something warm and hearty to go along with the cold leftovers from Sunday lunch. This is a basic recipe to which a cook might add any leftover meats and/or vegetables on hand to round out the meal. When adding leftovers directly to the soup, make sure that they are not strongly flavored or spiced. Simply prepared vegetables, like steamed peas and carrots, would make a particularly nice addition. On the other hand, a rich and pungent ratatouille would overpower the mixture. Leftover roast chicken can be sliced and served cold on the side or the meat shredded into the soup. A roast of any meat or game could be used in the same manner.

There is an old French tradition of faire chabrot that is meant for this dish. In French, the expression literally means "to clean the bowl." So to follow tradition, leave a bit of soup in the bottom of the bowl, add a light splash of red wine, and vigorously swirl the plate. Then, drink it up. It is a delicious end to a marvelous meal.

½ cup dry Tarbais beans (You can use any dry white bean as a substitute, like great northern or cannellini.)

¼ cup duck fat

5 medium leeks, white part only, washed and sliced crosswise

3 medium onions, peeled and cut into ¼-inch dice

1 head garlic, cloves separated and peeled

¼ teaspoon coarse salt plus more to taste

5 medium turnips, peeled, trimmed, and cut into medium dice

5 carrots, peeled, trimmed, and cut into medium dice

2 large ripe tomatoes, washed and halved

1 head celery, white bottom half only, washed, and sliced crosswise into 1-inch pieces

1 small head savoy cabbage, washed and quartered

One 10-ounce piece pork rind, blanched

One 10-ounce piece slab bacon, blanched

Approximately 2 quarts water or Bouillon de Poule (see page 282)

3 confit duck legs

2 medium potatoes, washed, peeled, and cubed

6 ounces haricots verts, washed and trimmed

½ bay leaf

Freshly ground black pepper to taste

1 tablespoon chopped fresh flat-leaf parsley

1 clove garlic, peeled and chopped

I   Place the Tarbais beans in a bowl and cover them with cold water by two inches. Soak for 12 hours. Drain and discard the water, reserving the beans.

2   Place the duck fat in a 3- to 4-quart heavy bottomed Dutch oven at least 4½ inches deep over low heat. Add the leeks, onions, and head of garlic and sauté for about 5 to 7 minutes or until the vegetables have sweat their liquid and are soft and translucent taking care that they do not brown. Add the ¼ teaspoon salt. Cover and cook for 3 to 4 minutes to extract additional water from the vegetables. Add the turnips, carrots, tomatoes, celery, cabbage, pork rind, and slab bacon along with reserved beans. Add enough water or Bouillon de Poule (or equal parts of each) to cover the vegetables by 2 inches. Raise the heat and bring to boil. Lower the heat and simmer, uncovered, for 50 to 60 minutes or until the vegetables are tender. Every 10 to 15 minutes, using a slotted spoon, skim off any scum or impurities that rise to the surface.

3   Add the confit, potatoes, haricots verts and bay leaf, and continue to simmer for about 15 minutes or until the slab bacon and potatoes are tender. Remove from the heat. Using a slotted spoon remove and discard the pork rind. Remove the slab bacon and confit duck legs and reserve them in a bowl. Place a clean damp kitchen towel over the bacon and duck to keep it from drying out.

4   Pour the soup through a fine sieve, straining the liquid back into the Dutch oven. Reserve the vegetables.

5   Using a food mill, process the vegetables to a thick, grainy puree. If you do not have a food mill, you can use a food processor or blender, but be sure to use the pulse setting so that the soup does not become a smooth puree. Transfer the vegetable puree to the liquid in the Dutch oven and stir to blend well.

6   Place the Dutch oven over medium heat and bring the soup to a boil. Season with salt and pepper to taste.

7   Peel the meat off of the duck legs and tear it into pieces. Slice the slab bacon. Place the duck meat and bacon in a sauté pan over medium-high heat. Add the parsley and chopped garlic clove and sauté for 4 to 5 minutes or until the meat is lightly browned and crisp.

9   Divide the meat among four soup plates. Ladle the hot soup over the meat and serve immediately.

SERVING SUGGESTION At my house this soup is always served family style in a tureen because it is the simplest way to do it. Place the meat in a warm soup tureen and ladle the puree over the meat. Heating the tureen will keep the soup warm longer.

Choux-fleur Suzanne

SUZANNE'S CAULIFLOWER

● SERVES 4

This is one of my favorite childhood dishes because I loved my mother's homemade mayonnaise. Cauliflower is okay; it has a very mild flavor and a nice crunchy texture, but for me, it was simply the best way to eat mayonnaise. Her addition of egg white makes the mayonnaise very light and creamy and, because the egg white dilutes the flavor somewhat, it is necessary to begin with a very flavorful mayonnaise. As far as I know it is her recipe, and like so many dishes she cooked I am not sure where it comes from. Because the vinegar acts as a bacteria-killing agent, I don't worry about using raw egg white. Additionally, most bacterial problems with raw eggs arise from the yolks, not the whites. It easily serves four, but I have been known to eat an entire head of cauliflower myself.

1 head cauliflower

1 teaspoon coarse salt plus more to taste

2 large egg whites

¾ cup Highly Seasoned Mayonnaise (see page 291)

1 tablespoon red wine vinegar

2 tablespoons Dijon mustard

Freshly ground pepper to taste

2 tablespoons finely chopped fresh flat-leaf parsley

I   Using a paring knife, trim off all the leaves from the bottom of the head of cauliflower. Trim off any stem that remains. Insert the tip of the knife into the bottom of the stem and remove the core of the stem. Wash the cauliflower under cold running water.

2   Place the whole cauliflower into a large saucepan with cold water to cover. Add 1 teaspoon salt and place over medium heat. Bring to a boil and cook for 15–20 minutes or until the core is tender when pierced with the point of a sharp knife. Remove from the heat and drain well. Place the cauliflower on a clean plate, cover and set aside in a cool place (or in the refrigerator) for 2 hours.

3   Place the egg whites in a clean bowl. Using an electric mixer or a whisk, whip them until they form stiff, shiny peaks.

4   Place the Highly Seasoned Mayonnaise into a small bowl. Fold the egg whites into the mayonnaise, add the vinegar and mustard, taste, and adjust seasoning with salt and pepper.

5   Place the cauliflower onto a serving plate. Pour the mayonnaise over the top and place in the refrigerator for at least 30 minutes or until well chilled. Remove from the refrigerator, sprinkle with parsley, and serve immediately.

Artichauts barigoules

ARTICHOKES WITH WHITE WINE AND HERBS

● SERVES 4

This is a fundamental recipe in the way that it teaches a cook how to develop and enhance the flavor of the artichokes by using olive oil and wine. The protein in the oil reinforces the artichoke flavor so that it is not lost during cooking. This idea is called "nourishing" in French cooking. The wine adds acidity, which keeps the artichokes from discoloring. This is the chemistry of the recipe, but I am certain that my mother simply learned to make it as a traditional dish. She made this as a side dish for poultry, veal, and sometimes even served it with fish.

Artichokes are generally served in the spring and summer, as this is when they are in season in France. I used to go with my mother to the market on the Boulevard de Strasbourg where there was a stand that sold only artichokes. There were many choices: small baby artichokes, big ones, green artichokes, and the purple artichokes from Provence. I like to use baby artichokes at the beginning of the season because they are very tender and have a wonderful flavor. All of these types of artichokes are now available in the United States, but you may have to go to a farmer's market or specialty food shop to find them.

If you would like to serve this dish warm, simply cover the cooked artichokes with aluminum foil and place them in an oven under low heat. Reduce the sauce as directed in the recipe and then pour the hot sauce over the warm artichokes and serve.

8 cups water

½ cup fresh lemon juice

20 baby artichokes

1 lemon, cut in half crosswise

3 tablespoons olive oil

5 cloves garlic, peeled and finely chopped

1½ medium onions (about 1½ cups), peeled and chopped into ¼-inch dice

1 bulb fennel, white part only, cut into ¼-inch slices

1 carrot, peeled and cut into ¼-inch dice

Coarse salt to taste

Freshly ground pepper to taste

2 sprigs fresh thyme

6 ounces slab bacon, cut into 1-inch dice and blanched

1 cup dry white wine

2 cups Bouillon de Poule (see page 282)

1   Combine the water and lemon juice in a mixing bowl.

2   Working with one artichoke at a time, *tourner* (to cut vegetables into the traditional slightly-faceted oval shape required in classic French cooking), and immediately rub the cut parts with the cut side of a lemon half to keep the artichoke flesh from discoloring. Quickly transfer the tournéed artichokes to the lemon water to prevent oxidation.

3   Heat the olive oil in a 3- to 4-quart braising pan at least 5 inches deep over medium heat. Add the garlic, onion, fennel, and carrot, stirring to coat well. Add salt and pepper to taste. Add the thyme and sauté for 5 minutes or until the vegetables have sweat their liquid and are soft, taking care that they do not brown.

4   Add the bacon and cook for an additional 5 minutes, taking care that it does not brown.

5   Drain the artichokes and pat them dry with a paper towel. Add them to the vegetables and cook, stirring occasionally, for 5 minutes.

6   Add the wine and, using a wooden spoon, stir to deglaze the pan. Bring to a simmer. Simmer, stirring frequently, for 5 minutes or until the liquid is reduced by half.

7   Add the bouillon and again bring to a simmer. Gently simmer, adjusting the heat if necessary, for 10 to 15 minutes or until the artichoke hearts are tender when pierced with the point of a sharp knife.

8   Using a slotted spoon, remove the artichokes from the braising liquid and put them into a bowl. Place a damp paper towel over the artichokes to prevent them from drying out.

9   Return the remaining ingredients to a gentle simmer. Cook for about 5 minutes or until the liquid is reduced by half. Remove from the heat and allow to cool for about 45 minutes or until the sauce is room temperature.

10 Place the artichokes in a single layer in a shallow serving bowl. Pour the sauce over the artichokes, cover and refrigerate overnight.

11 Remove from refrigerator, uncover, and serve, family style, directly from the bowl.

SERVING SUGGESTION This makes a wonderful main course for a light lunch, or it can be served as a side dish with grilled poultry or chops.

Fagot d'écrevisses des

BOILED CRAYFISH

ruisseaux de l'Aveyron

● SERVES 4

During the summer my dad and I usually visited my Grandmother Louise in Vezin, a small village in Aveyron. While there, it was our ritual to try to catch crayfish in the brook near her house. The day before our fishing trip my dad would buy a lamb's head from the local butcher shop. A lamb's head was the perfect crayfish trap because it was cheap, not too big, and most importantly it has a lot of holes and crevices for the crayfish to go into and some meat for them to eat. We would tie it up with string and plunge it into the brook, leaving it until the following day. When we returned, if we were lucky, we would find dozens of crayfish attached to the lamb's head. We would pull them off and put them into a bag or basket to carry them home.

Back at home, Grandma would have a big pot of boiling salted water ready for the crayfish. As soon as we arrived, she would quickly cook the crayfish and we would then eat them along with boiled potatoes sprinkled with coarse salt and smothered in my grandma's homemade mayonnaise. Because the crayfish were so fresh, they had a very sweet flavor and a little touch of the minerals from the river water. Even though we used a lamb's head to catch them, they never had a lamb flavor. Their warm and sweet flavor combined with the cold creamy mayonnaise was wonderful. Quel régal! (Fit for a king!)

3 tablespoons coarse salt

4 pounds crayfish

Mayonnaise (see page 291) to taste

2 pounds new or Red Bliss potatoes, boiled with the skin on

Unsalted butter to taste

Sea salt to taste

Freshly ground pepper to taste

1   Fill a 6- to 8-quart saucepan about 12 inches in diameter with cold water, leaving about 1½ inches at the top. Place over high heat, add salt and bring to a boil.

2   When the water is at a rapid boil, plunge one pound of crayfish into the water. Boil for about 2 to 4 minutes or until they are bright red. Using a slotted spoon, remove the crayfish from the water and drain well in a colander. Repeat, using the same water, until all the crayfish are cooked. (When cooking a large batch of shellfish, it is best to cook them in small amounts so that they will cook quickly and evenly. If the pot is too crowded the ones at the bottom will be overcooked before the ones at the top are finished.)

3   Serve hot with cold Mayonnaise on the side for dipping and a dish of hot potatoes. Season the potatoes to taste with butter, salt, and pepper.

SERVING SUGGESTION My favorite way to eat this dish is to serve it very simply. Spread brown paper or newspaper onto the kitchen table and put the crayfish in a pile in the middle of the table. Serve hot boiled new potatoes in a dish on the side, along with bowls of mayonnaise, butter, and sea salt. Peel the crayfish and dip them into the mayonnaise as you eat them. Spread butter onto the potatoes and sprinkle them with salt. You can either eat them with a knife and fork or pick them up and eat them as you would an apple.

NOTE My grandmother never cleaned the crayfish but I think that it is better to do so. If you choose to clean them, remove the black vein that runs along the spine before cooking. To make this task easier, put the crayfish in the freezer for about 5 to 10 minutes to put them to sleep. Be careful not to freeze them! Pick up a crayfish and hold it in the middle of the body so that it curves toward you. On the tail there are three small fins; take the middle fin between your thumb and index finger, twist and pull upward. The vein is attached to it and should come out along the spine when pulled.

La poule au pot et sa

CHICKEN IN A POT WITH

garniture de choux, carrotes,

STUFFING AND VEGETABLES

et son farci à la cansalade

● SERVES 4

This is a very old dish from the southwest of France. As all French schoolchildren learn, in 1600 the good king of France, Henri IV, and his first minister suggested that the population of France should have la poule au pot every Sunday. I think the reason they suggested it is because a "chicken in the pot" is a fête on the table and it warms the heart and soul.

My version of this traditional recipe came from my grandmother Marie Louise. She used to prepare the farce (stuffing) a day before so that all of the ingredients could really blend together and share their flavors. This dish, in particular, is why I developed my love and passion for food. The smell and the flavor were unbelievable. She would make it once or twice a month and only on Sundays. My first vivid memories of this are from when I was eight years old. I would open the door to the house and the smell of it cooking was so thick in the air that I could have eaten just the smell. We would arrive at noon and the chicken would have been cooking already for a few hours. The entire house smelled of the dish, not only chicken, but I could smell the carrots and celery and the meat of the farce. The bouillon, with its rich amber color and deep flavor, was always perfect. As it is a copious meal, there are usually some leftovers. The recipe for Bouillon de Poule aux Vermicelles (see page 37) follows this and is an excellent suggestion for leftovers.

16 ounces fresh pork belly, ground or finely chopped

4 ounces fresh foie gras, cleaned, deveined, and cut into 1-inch cubes

1 chicken liver, ground or finely chopped

1 chicken heart, ground or finely chopped

1 chicken gizzard, ground or finely chopped

5 cloves garlic, peeled and coarsely chopped

1 shallot, peeled and coarsely chopped

½ bunch fresh flat-leaf parsley leaves, chopped

5 large eggs

3 tablespoons heavy cream

2 tablespoons coarse salt plus more to taste

Freshly ground pepper to taste

2 slices country bread, crust removed, cut into 1-inch cubes

One 4- to 5-pound chicken, poularde, or young hen

1 gallon Bouillon de Poule (see page 282)

4 medium Idaho potatoes, peeled and quartered

2 hearts celery, washed, cut lengthwise, and blanched

1 small savoy cabbage, washed, quartered, and blanched

1 medium onion, peeled and cut in half

1½ pounds (about 5 large) carrots, peeled, trimmed, quartered lengthwise, and blanched

1 pound (about 6) leeks, white part only, washed and blanched

½ pound small white turnips, peeled, trimmed, and blanched

Bouquet Garni (see page 293)

½ head garlic, blanched

1   Combine the pork belly, foie gras, liver, heart, gizzard, chopped garlic, shallots, and parsley in a 2-quart mixing bowl.

2   Whisk together the eggs and heavy cream until well blended. Season with salt and pepper to taste. Add the bread and toss to coat well. Add the bread mixture to the meat mixture and mix thoroughly.

3   Salt and pepper the cavity of the chicken and fill the cavity with the stuffing.

4   To truss the chicken (see photo page 262), lay a piece of butcher's twine on the counter. Place the chicken on top with the neck facing you and the twine passing under the legs. Press the legs downward toward the counter to almost fold the legs underneath the body. Cross the twine over the top of the body, pulling tightly to close the opening. Pass the twine around the ends of the legs and pull each piece along the sides of the body. Fold the skin from the neck over the opening and tie the twine tightly over the skin of the neck and place it on a platter. Cover the chicken with a damp clean kitchen towel or paper towel and refrigerate overnight. It is important for the stuffing to infuse the chicken with all the flavors. Do not worry about any bacteria or salmonella, because the chicken will be poached for over 2 hours.

5   Remove the chicken from the refrigerator and place in a large stockpot. Add enough bouillon to cover it by 2 inches. Add 2 tablespoons of salt. Place the stockpot over medium heat and bring to a boil. Reduce the heat and gently simmer for 1 hour, skimming any scum or impurities that rise to the surface every 10 to 15 minutes.

6   Add the potatoes, celery, cabbage, onions, carrots, leeks, turnips, Bouquet Garni, and garlic, and continue to simmer for 40 minutes.

7   Using tongs or a large spatula, remove the chicken from the pot to a cutting board. Remove the string and scoop out the stuffing into a serving bowl. Transfer the chicken to a deep serving platter.

8   Strain the stock through a fine sieve into a soup terrine (or pitcher) and, if necessary, adjust the seasoning with salt and pepper. Place the vegetables around the chicken on the platter.

9   Pour the bouillon over the chicken and vegetables or serve it on the side in the soup tureen or pitcher. Serve the stuffing on the side. Alternately, to make individual servings, carve the chicken into eight pieces. Divide among four large soup plates. Add one piece of each vegetable and ¼ of the stuffing, and pour bouillon over the top.

Bouillon de poule

CHICKEN BOUILLON WITH NOODLES

aux vermicelles

● SERVES 4

This was a soup we would often have for Sunday night supper after we had eaten a Poule Au Pot (see page 34) for lunch. The Poule Au Pot was very filling and rich and we would always be full for hours afterwards. But since there was usually leftover bouillon and sometimes a little chicken and stuffing, it would provide us with a little light dinner later in the evening. As we never let anything go to waste, my grandmother would heat the leftover bouillon and add some pasta to make a warm and satisfying light supper.

4 ounces angel hair pasta

6 cups Bouillon de Poule (see page 282)

1   Preheat the oven to 200°F and place four ovenproof soup plates on the center rack to warm.

2   Bring salted water to a boil in a 6- to 8-quart stockpot over high heat. Add the pasta and cook according to package directions until tender.

3   Bring the bouillon to a simmer in a medium saucepan over medium heat.

4   Pour an equal amount of Bouillon de Poule into each of your warm soup plates. Add an equal amount of pasta into each soup plate and serve.

NOTE   If you want to serve this family style, combine the hot bouillon and cooked pasta in a soup tureen and serve it at the table.

Coq au vin

BRAISED CHICKEN IN RED WINE

● SERVES 4

When I was growing up almost everyone in my family had a chicken coop in the back yard to raise chickens, roosters, and eggs to eat. The roosters always fascinated me because they seemed so majestic with their proud stance and brightly colored cockscombs. Roosters have dark meat with a much more intense flavor than that from chickens. It is almost gamy. This dish is best when it is made with a 2-year-old rooster because older poultry has an even stronger flavor. The meat also tends to be tougher and more sinewy. To make the dark meat tender and succulent, it is marinated in a rich bodied, tannic red wine for four days. Because of the marinating, advance planning is required to make the dish, but it is a very easy dish to do and produces delicious results. I really do urge you to set aside a little time to prepare this wonderfully flavored traditional recipe.

The meat will not spoil during the 4-day marination in the refrigerator because of the cold temperature and the preserving qualities of the alcohol in the wine. Slow braising for 3 hours infuses even more flavor into the meat as well as breaks down the tough fibers to make it fork tender. Because the gamy meat has such a strong character it stands up very well to this long process. I suggest that you read through this recipe a couple of times so that you are comfortable with the cooking and finishing process. Don't be put off by the length of the recipe, I guarantee that it is really quite simple to execute once you get the method set.

3½ pounds boneless beef chuck (shoulder), cut into 1½-inch height by 1½-inch width

    by 3½-inch length

8 cups red wine

½ cups Armagnac

Bouquet Garni (see page 293)

Coarse salt to taste

3 ounces pork fat or lard, cut into 1-inch cubes

3 medium onions, peeled, coarsely chopped

1½ pounds slab bacon, blanched and cut into julienne

10 cloves garlic, peeled

1 Sprig thyme

2 Tablespoons flour

5 medium carrots, peeled, cut in half lengthwise, then cut into 3-inch-long sticks

¼ pound pork rind, blanched

2 tablespoons chopped fresh flat-leaf parsley

1   Spread the beef cubes out in an even layer in a large glass baking dish or nonreactive roasting pan. Pour 4 cups of the red wine and the Armagnac over the meat. Add the Bouquet Garni. Wrap the entire pan with plastic film and refrigerate for 2 days.

2   Strain the meat from the liquid through a fine sieve, separately reserving the marinating liquid and Bouquet Garni.

3   Pat the meat dry with paper towels and season generously with salt.

4   Preheat oven to 350°F.

5   In an 11-inch diameter by 5½-inch high braising pan, heat 1-ounce lard. Add onions; sweat for 1 to 2 minutes. Add bacon; sweat for 5 minutes. Add garlic.

6   In a 12-inch sauté pan, heat remaining 2 ounces lard over medium-high heat. Sauté meat until browned.

7   Add the meat to the onions in the braising pan. Add the Bouquet Garni and thyme. Add the flour. Cook gently for 3 minutes over low heat.

8   Add the remaining 4 cups of wine. Let reduce for 5 minutes over low heat. Add 3 cups of the marinating liquid. Let simmer for 5 minutes. Add the carrots, and blanched pork rind. Cover, and cook in oven (reduce temperature to 325°F) for 1½ hours. Uncover for remaining 2 hours. The meat should be tender, almost falling apart.

9   The meat should always be covered by liquid. Add water or more marinating liquid if needed. Skim off and discard any impurities that rise to the surface.

10 Spoon the daube into a large serving bowl or soup tureen and sprinkle with chopped parsley.

SERVING SUGGESTIONS I like to serve Pommes Purée (see page 294) with this dish. You can either serve the potatoes separately, put the daube on top of the potatoes, or try my favorite way—I put a big spoonful into my bowl of daube and let them dissolve a little into the sauce. A loaf of country bread to dunk in the sauce is always a good idea!

Boeuf en daube PAGE 50

Fricassée de cèpes bordelaise PAGE 20

La poule au pot et sa garniture de choux, carrotes et son farci à la cansalade PAGE 34

Cassoulet PAGE 46

Choux-fleur Suzanne
PAGE 27

Carré de porc aux pruneaux, endives braisées PAGE 53

Carré de porc aux pruneaux

ROAST PORK LOIN WITH PRUNES

● SERVES 4

This was a very special dish characteristic of the Sunday dinners of my childhood. Usually served in the fall or winter, I would know that it was going to be on the menu when I saw my mother or grandmother place the prunes to marinate in Armagnac. It remains a favorite dish of my family and was once featured in The New York Times *almost unchanged from the recipe cooked in the home kitchens of my childhood.*

2 cups pitted prunes

1 cup Armagnac

One 4½-pound boneless pork loin, all silver skin removed

Coarse salt to taste

Freshly ground pepper to taste

¾ cup duck fat or vegetable oil

2 large tomatoes, peeled, cored, seeded, and cubed

2 large carrots, peeled and chopped

2 cups chopped onions

3 teaspoons minced garlic

1 sprig fresh thyme

1 bay leaf

½ cup dry white wine

3½ cups veal stock

¼ cup clarified butter

4 endives, trimmed and blanched

1   Two days before you are ready to roast the pork, place the prunes in a nonreactive bowl with Armagnac to cover by about ½ inch. Cover with plastic film and refrigerate until ready to use. (The prunes can be marinated for up to 4 days; longer and they will begin to break down.)

2   Using a sharp knife, make a 2½- to 3-inch-deep cut running lengthwise down the center of the pork loin. Open the loin just as you would a book. Lay the prunes down the center of the open loin, one on top of the other, to make a neat row. Fold the meat over the prunes and, using kitchen twine, carefully tie the loin into a neat roll, spacing the loops about 2 inches apart all around the loin. Generously season the outside of the meat with salt and pepper.

3   Preheat the oven to 400°F.

4   Heat the duck fat in a large, ovenproof, heavy-duty skillet over medium heat. Add the pork loin and sear, turning frequently, until nicely browned on all sides. Lower the heat and add the tomatoes along with one half of the carrots, onions, and garlic to the skillet. Sauté for about 5 minutes or just until the vegetables are soft but have not taken on any color. Add the thyme and bay leaf and the wine and, using a wooden spoon, stir to deglaze the pan. Raise the heat to medium and simmer for about 5 minutes or until the wine is reduced by half. Add 2 cups of the veal stock and place in the preheated oven. Roast, basting with the liquid in the skillet every 10 minutes, for 30 minutes.

5   Lower the oven temperature to 375°F and roast the pork, basting every 15 minutes, for an additional hour or until the juices run clear when the meat is pierced with a sharp knife or until 145°F is reached on an instant-read thermometer. Add water as needed to keep the braising liquid from getting too thick or evaporating entirely. You want it to remain quite juicy.

6   About 30 minutes before the pork is ready, prepare the endives. Heat the clarified butter in a large sauté pan over medium-high heat. Add the endives and sauté for about 10 minutes or until golden on all sides. Season with salt and pepper to taste and remove from the heat. Set aside.

7   Heat the remaining duck fat in a large, ovenproof skillet with low sides over very low heat. Add the remaining onion, carrot, and garlic and sauté for about 5 minutes, or just until the vegetables are soft but have not taken on any color. Place the reserved endives on top of the soft vegetables. Add the remaining 1½ cups of veal stock and place in the oven. Bake, basting occasionally, for about 20 minutes or until the endives are tender, nicely glazed, and golden brown. Remove from the oven. Taste and, if necessary, adjust the seasoning with salt and pepper. Set aside and keep warm.

8   Remove the pork from the skillet and place on a warm platter. Tent lightly with aluminum foil to keep warm.

9   Place the skillet over medium heat and simmer the braising liquid for 8 minutes or until reduced slightly. Pour through a fine sieve into a gravy boat and set aside.

10 Place the endives in the center of a serving platter. Remove the twine from the pork and, using a sharp knife, cut the meat, crosswise, into ¾-inch-thick slices. Place the prune-filled pork slices over the endives and serve with the sauce passed on the side.

Tarte aux pommes

MOM'S APPLE TART

bonne Maman

SERVES 6

When my mom would make this, it was the first sign of fall and the end of summer vacation because she would make it only when the apples were being picked at the local orchards. Apples that have just been picked have a crisp fresh flavor that just isn't there when they have been stored for several months. Even today, in my restaurant kitchen or at home, apple desserts still signal the beginning of fall.

I always loved (and still do) the combination of the two textures of the fresh apple and the apple compote. The compote is a very concentrated flavor and the texture is soft and comforting like baby food. The fresh slices of apple complement this with a firm texture and crisp flavor. To me, it always tastes best when it is still warm.

Pastry dough for an 8-inch tart (see page 298), chilled

1 large egg, lightly beaten

2 Golden Delicious apples

2 cups Apple Compote (see page 295)

2 tablespoons unsalted butter, melted

3 tablespoons confectioners' sugar

3 tablespoons apricot jam

1   Roll out the chilled pastry dough to a ¼-inch-thick round on a lightly floured surface. Line an 8-inch tart shell with the pastry dough. Gently press the dough into the corners of the tart shell and, using a paring knife, trim off the excess dough around the rim of the shell. Place in the refrigerator for 30 minutes to chill.

2   Preheat the oven to 325°F.

3   Remove the pastry shell from the refrigerator and line it with waxed or parchment paper. Place dry beans or baking weights on the lined shell. Place the tart shell on a cookie sheet in the preheated oven and bake for 15 to 20 minutes or until it has a dry surface and a pale color. Remove the pastry shell from the oven. While it is still hot, remove the beans (or weights) and the paper and, using a pastry brush, lightly coat the inside of the shell with the beaten egg. Set aside to cool completely before filling.

4   Peel and core the apples. Cut them in half and then into ⅛-inch-thick slices.

5   Spoon the Apple Compote into the shell, smoothing it out with a spatula to an even layer.

6   Starting on the outside edge of the shell, lay the apple slices on top of the compote, slightly overlapping the slices as you make a ring around the edge of the tart shell. When you have finished the outside ring, continue making rings until the entire surface of the tart is covered with neatly arranged apple slices. Brush the apples with the melted butter and sprinkle confectioners' sugar over the top, making sure that the apples are well sugared.

7   Cover the pastry edges of the tart with strips of aluminum foil to protect the pastry from overcooking and burning. Place the tart on a cookie sheet.

8   Raise the oven temperature to 350°F. Place the tart in the oven and bake for 30 minutes or until the apple slices are translucent and their edges are lightly browned. At the 10-minute and 20-minute marks, using a pastry brush, coat the tart with some of the remaining melted butter, and sprinkle with some of the remaining confectioner's sugar. Remove the tart from the oven and place on a wire rack.

9   Place the apricot jam in a small saucepan over low heat. Heat, stirring constantly, for 2 to 3 minutes until it is liquefied. Strain through a fine mesh sieve into a bowl. While the tart is still warm, using a clean pastry brush, carefully glaze the top with the melted apricot jam.

10 Cool the tart for 15 to 20 minutes, then brush the top again with the apricot jam. If the jam has solidified, re-warm it for 2 to 3 minutes.

11 Serve the tart while it is still warm.

Soufflé au chocolat

DARK CHOCOLATE SOUFFLÉ

● SERVES 4

When I was young and would come home from school around 4 o'clock in the afternoon, I used to have a bar of chocolate on a slice of buttered bread. It was my favorite goûter or after-school snack. We always had this dark chocolate in the kitchen and one day my mother decided to try making a chocolate soufflé with it. Her creation was delicious. She made her soufflés in the old-fashioned way, which means to start with a pastry cream. The pastry cream had egg yolks and flour in it, which added strength to the soufflé so it would not collapse. It is a foolproof trick to use. The result was a soufflé that had a heavier texture, closer to an underbaked or very moist cake. As a child I loved this texture but now I prefer a soufflé that is lighter. This recipe is my interpretation. The key ingredient and the star in this recipe is the chocolate. I love bitter chocolate because the chocolate flavor is not diluted by the addition of sugar and milk. Dark chocolate stands up to the sugars in the recipe and keeps its deep flavor.

I use a mixing bowl over a pot of boiling water instead of a double boiler. This is much more efficient because you are not transferring the batter from bowl to double boiler to bowl. By using a makeshift double boiler, you save time during the cooking and there are fewer bowls to wash.

2 tablespoons unsalted butter plus more to coat molds

1 tablespoon sugar plus more to coat molds

9 ounces dark chocolate, chopped

4 large egg yolks

10 large egg whites

Pinch salt

1   Preheat the oven to 400°F.

2   Butter and sugar four 6-ounce soufflé molds.

3   Bring a medium saucepan of water to a simmer over medium heat.

4   Combine the chocolate and the 2 tablespoons butter in a stainless steel mixing bowl. Place the mixing bowl over the pot of simmering water to create a double boiler effect and, stirring constantly, gently melt the chocolate and butter together. Be sure that no water gets into the bowl and that the chocolate does not burn or bubble.

5   Remove the bowl from the heat and dry the bottom. Whisk in the egg yolks and set aside.

6   Using an electric mixer or a whisk, beat the egg whites until they are frothy, then add a pinch of salt. Add the tablespoon of sugar and continue beating until soft peaks form.

7   Using a spatula, fold ⅓ of the egg whites into the chocolate mixture. Gently fold half of the chocolate mixture into the remaining egg whites; then, fold the mixture into the remaining chocolate. Be careful not to overmix the batter and deflate the egg whites.

8   Fill each soufflé mold to within ⅛ inch of the top. Place the molds on a baking sheet in the preheated oven and bake for 6 minutes. When finished, the risen soufflé should be set and the center just soft to the touch.

9   Using a large metal spatula or tongs, transfer each hot soufflé to a serving plate. Serve immediately.

Riz au lait

Marie Louise

● SERVES 6

This dessert is a standing ovation to my grandmother. Riz au lait literally means rice and milk. It is not exactly rice pudding in the traditional sense because the final texture is more like a soup than a custard. I used to sit in the kitchen and watch my grandmother make this dessert. While I watched her stirring the pot, the expression on her face was one of love and pride. She knew that her cooking would make all of us very happy. Everyone in the family loved this dessert and so she would make it frequently, almost every Sunday. Even though she made it once a week, I never tired of eating it. I can assure you that there were never any leftovers! Just remember, it is very important that this be cooked very, very slowly or it will be runny rather than thick and soupy. It took my grandmother about 6 hours to make!

¾ cup long-grain Carolina rice

1 small bay leaf

2 cups plus 2 tablespoons water

6 cups milk

1 cup sugar

1 vanilla bean, cut in half

in me during my years at hotel school that I am able to give classical French cooking my own stamp. When you are taught to understand the defined principles of taste, it is a simple jump to expanding on those principles.

Basic techniques and formulas are fundamental to the kitchen, just as a foundation is to a building. Once you have the solid base, you can construct a simple house or a château. I believe that the standardization of a technical school goes much further toward creating a well-rounded cook able to adapt to whatever presents itself in the course of a demanding career in the kitchen than does working up through the ranks of many different kitchens. Of course, the ideal is to go to a culinary or hotel school while working in your area of interest so that, as a cook, you are able to combine lessons with practical knowledge on a daily basis.

As a part of our training we had to work in a variety of places to expose us to the reality of the profession. It was important that we have the training and discipline to endure the expectations of a well-run kitchen. We learned about food theory, nutrition, sanitation, personal hygiene, the rules of profitability, organization, and the finances (*bon d'économat*) of running an efficient kitchen. We learned both the front and the back of the house, but in the end I chose the kitchen. I always did very well in my cooking classes, gaining high marks. I was not always so good at my other studies, as I often read cookbooks during my accounting classes. However, I was good enough in math to do my food costs correctly!

Sometimes I would practice cooking at home. I remember making Canard à l'Orange (see page 86) and simple things like pizzas and quiche. My mom always let me have the kitchen, though sometimes she would look over my shoulder and make suggestions. Sometimes I agreed and sometimes not. She would often laugh a little while watching me because I was so serious and I used so many pots and pans. When I would serve my dishes, my family was always complimentary and very encouraging.

I worked in a restaurant in the Pyrenees on the *Axle* road *Foix-Ax Les Thermes* named *Les Charmilles*. The region was famous for its native trout. At the restaurant, we kept live trout in a small pool and when someone ordered a trout dish I would go out back, pick one up, kill it with the back of my knife handle, and clean it. One of our specialties was trout meuniére (see page 84) braised in créme fraîche and almonds. This was an example of a simple basic technique, *meuniére* (floured fish or organ meats, fried in butter, and garnished with lemon juice, browned butter, and parsley), taken to another level as it was braised in the créme fraîche and almonds. The final result would never have been so wonderful without an understanding of the basic recipe.

Another reality of the profession that I experienced only when I began my work in restaurants was the grueling routine of long hours on my feet as I spent the day doing the basic preparation chores and then standing up to the speed of service and the pressure of performing under fire. I did not expect restaurant life to be so hard. Everything was rushed and you had to cope at very high speeds—even idling was at high speed! If you weren't well organized and prepared, your station would fall apart and affect the whole kitchen. It was much more intense than I had ever imagined.

I realized that going to school and working in a restaurant gave me an intense challenge that only served to generate my determination to become a fine chef. In fact,

my determination grew into an obsession, which I believe gave me the strength and desire to stick to my plan even when the going got tough. This stick-to-it-iveness is, I think, one of the most important keys to longevity in the career of any chef.

I remember my final exam in school as though it were yesterday. We went into the kitchen and everyone pulled two recipes out of a hat. I got Filet de Sole Bonne Femme (see page 82) and Poulet Grillé à la Diable (see page 89). We then wrote out our list of ingredients on a *bon d'économat* to get the necessary supplies. We had to list all of the ingredients in grams and calculate the food costs in prices by kilo. We had to organize and collect the ingredients by recipe and then prepare the dish for four people. There was also a written exam. Fortunately, I did well and passed with flying colors.

I still lived at home but, at sixteen, I was expected to go right from school to a job. My dad knew one of the managers at the Café de la Paix in Paris who put him in touch with the chef, Georges Buffeteau. A couple of weeks after my graduation, I was invited to come to work in Paris. I was terrified. School was quite insular and I wasn't sure that I was ready to jump from the frying pan into the fire. But I had no choice, so I packed my bags for a whole new life.

Crème Mulligatawny
CURRY SOUP WITH APPLES

Potage Parmentier
POTATO AND LEEK SOUP

Bouillon de Volaille à la Royale
CHICKEN BOUILLON WITH CUSTARD

Oeuf Cocotte
BAKED EGG WITH CREAM

Gnocchis à la Romaine
POLENTA GNOCCHIS

Champignons à la Grecque
COLD STEWED MUSHROOMS, GREEK STYLE

Sole Glacée Bonne Femme
GLAZED SOLE WITH MUSHROOMS

Truite aux Amandes les Charmilles
TROUT WITH ALMONDS AND CREAM

Canard Rôti à l'Orange
ROAST DUCK WITH ORANGE

Poulet Grillé à la Diable
GRILLED CHICKEN

Navarin d'Agneau Printanier
LAMB STEW WITH SPRING VEGETABLES

Blanquette de Veau à l'Ancienne
VEAL STEW

Pots de Crème
VANILLA CREAM CUSTARD

Glace à la Vanille aux Pruneaux
VANILLA ICE CREAM WITH ARMAGNAC PRUNES

Crème mulligatawny

CURRY SOUP WITH APPLES

• SERVES 4

Finding the right balance of flavor between the spicy curry, the crisp, tart apples, and the sweet onions in this soup is a real test for a cook. It can't be too hot, the tartness has to counterbalance the heat, and the sweetness has to introduce another level of flavor and give the aromatic soup a hint of sugar. When the right proportion is met among all three, a marvelous balance of flavor is created. I always make this soup a day ahead and refrigerate it overnight so that the flavors can mellow and come together to make the perfect blend. I find that chilling allows you to really taste the complexity of the soup.

½ cup plus 2 tablespoons light olive oil

2 onions, peeled and chopped

5 Granny Smith apples, peeled, cored, and sliced

¼ teaspoon coarse salt plus more to taste

3 tablespoons mild curry powder

3 tomatoes cored, peeled, seeded, and quartered

3 cups water

3 cups Bouillon de Poule (see page 282)

2 cloves garlic, peeled

1½ tablespoons shredded unsweetened coconut

Freshly ground pepper to taste

1 cup hot lightly brewed black tea

1 teaspoon dried currants

8 celery leaves

1 Golden Delicious apple, peeled, halved, and sliced, length-wise, paper-thin

1 stalk celery, finely diced

½ cup heavy cream

5 tablespoons Tomato Confit (see page 292), coarsely chopped

1. Heat 2 tablespoons oil in a large pot with a cover over medium heat. Add the onions and sauté for 5 minutes or until they have sweat their liquid and are soft. Make sure they do not brown.

2. Add the Granny Smith apples and ¼ teaspoon salt. Cover and cook for 5 minutes to extract the water from the apples.

3. Add 2 tablespoons of the curry powder and cook, stirring constantly, for 4 minutes.

4. Add the tomatoes, water, and bouillon, and then the garlic and coconut and bring to a boil. Reduce the heat and gently simmer for 10 minutes or until the apples are tender.

5. Remove the soup from the heat. Place the soup in a blender and process until smooth. Strain the soup through a fine mesh sieve, discarding the solids.

6. Season with salt and pepper to taste. Cover and refrigerate overnight.

7. Heat ¼ cup of the remaining olive oil in a small saucepan over medium heat. Add the remaining 1 tablespoon of curry powder and cook, stirring constantly, for 5 minutes. Remove from the heat. Set aside to cool to room temperature.

8. Combine the tea and currants in a small bowl and let infuse for 15 to 20 minutes. Strain through a fine sieve, reserving the currants and discarding the tea.

9. Heat the remaining ¼ cup light olive oil in a small sauté pan over medium heat. Add the celery leaves and fry for about 2 minutes or until just wilted. Drain on paper towels and reserve.

10. Combine the Golden Delicious apples and celery with the reserved curry-flavored oil and currants.

11. Remove the soup from the refrigerator and whisk in the heavy cream until well blended. Place ¼ of the apple celery mixture in the center of each of four soup plates. If desired, you can use two spoons to shape the mixture into a quenelle. Place one quarter of the fried celery leaves on top of the apple mixture. Place one quarter of the tomato confit around each quenelle. Present the soup in a terrine at the table and carefully ladle it into the soup plates.

Potage parmentier

POTATO AND LEEK SOUP

○ SERVES 4

This soup is named for Antoine Parmentier, who was a great promoter of the potato in the late 1700s in France, and you will find that most recipes that have Parmentier in the title have potatoes as a component. At one point, potatoes were even called parmentières.

This is a fundamental recipe for two reasons. First, leek and potato soup is a base recipe for several other soups, such as watercress, nettle, and vichyssoise (which is simply a chilled version of the basic soup). Secondly, the method of cooking vegetables in bouillon and puréeing them to create a thick texture with a lot of flavor is a basic technique often used in French vegetable soups. The home cook, for speed and convenience, would more likely leave the vegetables in pieces in the broth.

5 tablespoons unsalted butter

6 medium leeks, white part only, washed and sliced lengthwise

1½ medium onions, peeled and sliced crosswise

¼ teaspoon coarse salt plus more to taste

1½ teaspoons all-purpose flour

3 cups Bouillon de Poule (see page 282)

3 cups water

1 Bouquet Garni (see page 293)

1½ pounds Idaho potatoes, peeled and cubed

2 tablespoons crème fraîche

Freshly ground pepper to taste

1. Heat 1½ tablespoons of the butter in a large pot with a cover over medium heat. Add the leeks and onions and sweat for 5 minutes or until they are soft, taking care that the vegetables do not brown. Add ¼ teaspoon salt and cover. Cook for 5 minutes to extract the water from the vegetables. Add the flour and cook for 5 minutes, stirring constantly.

2. Add the bouillon, water, and Bouquet Garni. Bring to a boil and cook for 5 to 10 minutes. Add the potatoes and bring again to a boil and cook for 5 minutes. Reduce the heat and simmer for 5 to 10 minutes or until the vegetables are very tender. Remove from heat and let the mixture cool for 15 to 20 minutes.

3. Using a blender or food mill, process the soup until smooth and silky in texture. Strain through a large-holed China cap or mesh sieve into a clean saucepan.

4. Place the saucepan over medium heat and bring the soup to a boil. Whisk in the crème fraîche along with the remaining butter and blend well. Taste and adjust the seasoning with salt and pepper. Serve hot.

SERVING SUGGESTION The smooth texture and mild flavor of this soup make an excellent background for other foods with more distinct taste. For instance, I often shave fresh black or white truffles over the top or add a garnish of cooked shrimp, crab, or lobster.

Bouillon de volaille

CHICKEN BOUILLON WITH CUSTARD

à la royale

○ | SERVES 4

This dish appears very simple but, in fact, was created to test the cook's abilities in making custard. The recipe uses bouillon instead of milk as the liquid, which, without any fat to add smoothness, makes it more difficult to achieve the perfect custardy texture. Milk provides proteins that bind the custard together, while in this case the texture is achieved through the cooking method, as bouillon has far less protein than milk. The use of the bouillon in the custard also accentuates the intense chicken flavor of the dish. The custard is refrigerated overnight to allow it to set and firm, and then it is cut, cold, to add to the soup.

1 tablespoon unsalted butter plus more to butter the baking dish

4⅓ cups Bouillon de Poule (see page 282)

2 pinches chopped fresh chervil

2 to 3 leaves chopped fresh tarragon

3 large egg yolks

1 large egg

Coarse salt to taste

Freshly ground pepper to taste

1   Preheat the oven to 325°F.

2   Lightly butter a 5" x 5" x 2" square baking dish.

2   Using 4 tablespoons of the butter, generously coat the bottom of an ovenproof baking dish. Set aside.

3   Pat the fish dry with a paper towel and season the inside with salt and pepper to taste.

4   Heat the oil in a large sauté pan over high heat until it is almost smoking. Add the trout and quickly brown both sides of each fish. It should take no longer than 2 minutes per side.

5   Place the browned trout in a single layer in the prepared baking dish. Spread 2 tablespoons of créme fraîche over each trout, making sure the entire surface is covered. Sprinkle almonds over the top of each trout and dot each fish with ¼ tablespoon of the remaining butter. Place the dish in the preheated oven and bake for about 10 minutes or until golden brown.

6   Remove from the oven and serve hot.

NOTE   When you buy your trout from the fishmonger, be sure to specify that you want them cleaned and boned, but whole and with the skin on. This means the back fins should be trimmed off and the bones and innards should be removed through a slit in the belly of the fish.

Canard rôti à l'orange

ROAST DUCK WITH ORANGE

● | SERVES 4

In this classic recipe, the sauce is made with a gastrique that has a base of sweet and acid cooked together until almost all of the liquid has evaporated. It is used specifically in sauce recipes for savory dishes that have fruit in them, like the classic duck with orange. A gastrique is used both as a base for sauces and as a basting glaze during cooking. Since duck is a very rich, fatty meat, the sauce must also be rich and flavorful to marry well with it. The sweetly acidic flavor of the orange is greatly enhanced by the Grand Marnier. This recipe is one where I learned about balancing the contrasting tastes of sweet (sugar) and sour (vinegar). This type of sauce is particularly well suited to fatty meats like pork, duck, and foie gras.

Coarse salt to taste

Freshly ground pepper to taste

One 5- to 6-pound Long Island or Pekin duck

3 tablespoons unsalted butter

1 lemon

3 oranges

¼ cup sugar

¼ cup red wine vinegar

5 blood oranges, juiced

2 cups Duck Jus (see page 287)

¼ cup Grand Marnier

1 tablespoon arrowroot or corn starch

6   Combine the carrots with 2 tablespoons of butter, 2 tablespoons of water, and 1 table-spoon of sugar in a small sauté pan over medium heat. Cook, stirring constantly, for about 5 minutes or until all of the water has evaporated and the sugar has dissolved. The carrots should be al dente and lightly glazed. If the carrots seem undercooked, add a tablespoon of water and continue to cook for another minute. Remove from the heat. Set aside, covered, to keep warm.

7   Repeat the same process to cook and reserve the turnips and the onions.

8   Combine the reserved sauce and meat over medium heat in a large sauté pan. Bring it to a simmer, lower the heat, and simmer for about 3 minutes to just heat through.

9   Bring a medium saucepan of salted water to a boil over high heat. Plunge the haricots verts, fava beans, and peas into the boiling water for 2 minutes to just heat through. Drain well. Toss with the remaining 1 tablespoon of butter. Reserve and keep warm.

10 Transfer the meat and sauce to the center of a large serving platter. Distribute the veg-etables and potatoes evenly over the top and serve.

Blanquette de veau

à l'ancienne

SERVES 4

Blanquette is a classic veal preparation but it can also be made with fish and vegetables. The two key lessons here are how to prepare meat for cooking and how to make sauce. The meat is blanched first in water to remove the impurities; then it is cooked in light veal or chicken stock. The sauce starts with a base of a roux blanc (white roux), which is the combination of fat and flour. Done properly, a roux will effect a thickness and shine in sauces. Done poorly, the sauce will be lumpy and have a pasty flour taste. The sauce is finished with eggs and cream and then a tiny hint of fresh lemon juice to balance the creamy acidity and to add another layer of richness and texture. This is called a liaison and the action is to lier. In school, they would use shorthand and simply say "lier la sauce!"

Personally, I love to eat a blanquette (stew). I particularly like the contrast of the richness of the sauce with the tanginess of the acidity of the lemon. The meat should be extremely tender but not falling apart in the sauce. When the preparation is well executed, the meat is moist and cooked to perfection with a thick, deeply flavorful sauce. It is a dish that acknowledges the art of the saucier.

2½ pounds veal shoulder, cut into 2-inch cubes

1 cup dry white wine

3½ cups White Veal Stock (see page 285) or Bouillon de Poule (see page 282)

3 cloves garlic, peeled and halved

2 leeks, white part only, cut in half crosswise

1 onion, peeled and cut in half

1 carrot, peeled, trimmed, and halved lengthwise

Bouquet Garni (see page 293)

Coarse salt to taste

½ cup unsalted butter

¼ cup all-purpose flour

4 ounces white button mushrooms, trimmed of any dry spots

1 tablespoon plus a few drops fresh lemon juice

8 pearl onions, peeled and blanched

1 tablespoon sugar

2 tablespoons water

3 large egg yolks

1 cup heavy cream

Freshly ground pepper to taste

2 tablespoons chopped fresh flat-leaf parsley or chives

1   Place the veal cubes in a large pot with cold, salted water to cover by about an inch. Place over high heat and bring to a boil. Immediately, remove from the heat and drain in a colander. Rinse under cold running water, then pat dry with paper towels.

2   Place the blanched veal in a clean, large, heavy-bottomed saucepan. Add the white wine and place over medium-high heat. Bring to a boil, then lower the heat and simmer for 2 minutes. Add enough of the stock or bouillon to cover the veal by 1½ inches. Raise the heat and bring to a gentle boil. Lower the heat and simmer, occasionally skimming the impurities that rise to the top, for 25 minutes. Add the garlic, leeks, halved onion, carrots, Bouquet Garni, and a pinch of salt. Bring to a boil, then reduce the heat to a gentle simmer. Simmer for about 45 minutes or until the meat is fork tender. Every 10 minutes or so skim any fat or impurities that rise to the surface.

3   Using a slotted spoon, remove the meat from the cooking liquid and place it in a bowl. Cover with a damp towel to keep moist. Strain the liquid through a fine mesh sieve back into the pot, discarding the vegetables (or use them to make a light salad for lunch). Return the pot to the stove over medium heat and bring to a simmer. Simmer for about 5 to 10 minutes or until the liquid is reduced by somewhat less than half.

4   Melt 4 tablespoons of the butter in a large saucepan over low heat, stir in the flour, and cook, stirring constantly, for 5 minutes, making sure that the flour does not brown or color.

5   Whisk the hot, reduced, braising liquid into the roux. Place over medium-low heat and cook, whisking constantly, until the sauce has thickened. Lower the heat and cook, whisking constantly, for 10 minutes. Every 2 to 3 minutes, stir with a wooden spoon to keep the sauce from sticking to the bottom of the pan and burning. If the sauce seems to be too thick, thin with a little water or stock.

6   Melt 2 tablespoons of the remaining butter in a medium sauté pan with a cover over high heat. Add the mushrooms and 1 tablespoon lemon juice. Cover and cook for 1 to 2 minutes or until the mushrooms are al dente. Remove from the heat and let rest for 10 minutes. Drain and separately reserve the liquid and mushrooms.

7   Add the mushroom liquid to the sauce and return the sauce to medium heat. Cook, stirring constantly, for 3 minutes. Pass the sauce through a fine mesh sieve into a large clean saucepan. Add the veal and mushrooms and place over medium heat. Cook for about 3 minutes or just until the mixture is hot.

8   Combine the pearl onions and sugar with the water and remaining 2 tablespoons of butter in a small sauté pan over medium heat. Cook, stirring constantly, for about 5 minutes or until all the water has evaporated and the sugar has dissolved. The pearl onions should be al dente and lightly glazed. Remove from the heat. Cover and keep warm.

9   Beat the egg yolks and heavy cream in a small mixing bowl until well combined.

10   Remove the blanquette from the heat and whisk the egg mixture into it. Add the remaining few drops of lemon juice, taste, and, if necessary, adjust the seasoning with salt and pepper. Pour the blanquette into a serving dish. Distribute the pearl onions and parsley evenly over the top and serve.

Pots de crème

VANILLA CREAM CUSTARDS

● SERVES 4

This is a variation of crème renversée, which is a large custard that is unmolded onto a plate to be served family style. It is similar to a crème caramel. In this recipe, the custard is cooked in a little pot and served solo in its petit pot. When making crème renversée for dessert, my mom used to save some of the crème and cook it in a small pot, which I got to eat at 4 o'clock as an after-school snack or goûter.

You can make different flavored custards using this recipe as a base. For chocolate, add 2 teaspoons of cocoa and 2 additional teaspoons of sugar at Step 3. For coffee, whisk in 1½ teaspoons instant coffee at Step 4. Of course, do not forget to eliminate the vanilla bean from the recipe if you decide to change the flavor.

2 large egg yolks

1 large egg

¼ cup plus 2 teaspoons sugar

1¼ cups milk

½ vanilla bean, split

1   Preheat oven to 350°F.

2   Whisk together the 2 egg yolks, 1 whole egg, and sugar in a small mixing bowl until they are pale yellow and creamy.

3   Combine the milk and the vanilla bean in a small saucepan over medium heat and scald the mixture. (Bring just to a boil, the point where bubbles begin to form around the edge.) Remove from the heat and cool the milk for 5 minutes.

4   Remove and discard the vanilla bean. Whisk ¼ cup of the warm milk into the egg mixture to temper it, then add the remaining milk.

5   Evenly divide the mixture into 4 small ovenproof *pot de crème* cups.

6   Place the filled cups into a baking pan that is almost the same height as the cups. Carefully fill the pan halfway with boiling water, making sure you do not splash any water into the cups. Cover the entire pan with aluminum foil and place in the preheated oven. Bake for 30 minutes or until just set, noting that the pudding will continue to cook after removal from the oven.

7   Remove the cups from the water bath, and cool slightly on a wire rack; then refrigerate for at least 2 hours or until chilled. Serve cold.

Glace à la vanille

VANILLA ICE CREAM WITH ARMAGNAC PRUNES

aux pruneaux

● SERVES 4

The base is a rich vanilla ice cream into which prunes marinated in Armagnac are added. Crème anglaise is a basic recipe, which becomes ice cream when worked in an ice cream machine. Vanilla ice cream is also one of the most basic recipes I know. I can still remember the day that the pastry chef instructor decided to show us how to make a glace aux pruneaux for a special dinner event at the school. How we all loved those marinated prunes! Just remember, the prunes have to marinate for a week before you can make the glace.

2 cups whole pitted prunes

2 cups Armagnac

2 cups whole milk

2 cups heavy cream

1½ vanilla beans, split lengthwise

½ cup sugar

8 large egg yolks

I   Place the prunes into a glass jar or non-reactive container. Add the Armagnac, making sure the prunes are covered by ½ inch, and press plastic film on top of the prunes to keep them submerged in the liquor. Place in the refrigerator for a minimum of one week to marinate. (These can be stored, tightly covered and refrigerated, for up to 15 days.)

equivalent to seventy-five dollars a month, including a room. The room was a very small one with a slanted roof on the top floor of the Hôtel Scribe, which was attached to the Café. I lived by myself in this plain room with a tiny window and the usual hotel furniture of a bed, a nightstand, and a small table with a lamp.

Of course, I had no kitchen in the room, which was fine because I ate most of my meals at work or in cheap neighborhood bistros. One of my favorites was the Réstaurant Pour Ouvriers at Les Halles. Here you could eat like a king for a dollar. They served hearty, nourishing food; I often began with some *charcuterie*, followed by a veal chop and green beans, and a *crème renversée* for dessert. The meal even came with a small pitcher of wine to toast my good fortune.

For a young cook from the South, the Café was really something to experience. To me, it remains one of the most beautiful buildings in Paris. The buildings of the Café and Hôtel make a triangle and take up almost the entire block. Located right by the opera house at the Place de l'Opéra, it is bordered by the Boulevard des Capucines and rues Auber and Scribe. The architect Garnier built both the Opera and the Café during the reign of Napoleon III. Opened in 1862, the Café was inaugurated with an auspicious christening by the Empress Eugenie. A *côte de boeuf* with potato puree cost one and a half francs, which today is about sixteen cents. It seems so little but I'm sure it was a fortune in those days.

When I arrived at Café de la Paix, it was considered a very famous restaurant with two Michelin stars. It was owned by the Millon family, who also owned the Grand Hôtel on the Rue Scribe and the Maurice Hôtel, which was not far away on the Rue de Rivoli. The Café was divided into two parts: in front was the Salon de Thé where fashionable people sat in wicker chairs placed in a row facing the street, watching Paris pass by while they drank coffee and sipped aperitifs. The restaurant, with proper tables and banquettes, linen tablecloths, and waiters in bow ties and long white aprons, filled the back. It was decorated in the same Belle Epoque style that had been its fashion from the time it was built.

I would wake up early every morning and put on a clean uniform: navy blue and white checked cotton pants, a heavy white cotton chef's coat, and *Sabot* kitchen clogs. The hotel was just behind the Café and it was a nice walk down Rue Scribe to the Place de l'Opéra, particularly in the spring. The brisk walk was just long enough to wake me up.

The doorway to the kitchen was on Place de l'Opéra, between the end of the outdoor café and the entrance to the bar. I walked down the two flights of stairs into the kitchen. You could feel the heat of the coal stoves from the kitchen as you entered, and on a quiet morning you could hear the subway rumbling. Next to the stairs was a platform that went up and down like an open elevator, which was how deliveries were sent down into the kitchen.

I was put at the sauce station to work for the chef *saucier,* Charles Lejay. Chef Lejay was in his fifties and had a very hard personality, but I quickly understood that he knew everything about being a *cuisinier* and how to set up and organize the kitchen. He was tall and thin, with a little pot belly. His hair was gray-white and he kept it very short, almost like a military haircut. He had a nice face, not handsome but pleasant, that belied his personality. All day long, in between his yelling and ordering, he would tell me war stories. He had fought in the Second World War as a rear-gunman in fighter planes and had gone on from the brigade of the military to the brigade of the kitchen. I think the discipline and hard work of the kitchen suited him. Even though he had a son and his military career, the kitchen was his entire life.

When I got to the kitchen it was usually very quiet. We, the *commis*, started at 8 o'clock and the *chefs de partie* didn't start coming in until nine. Each morning would find a fresh 2 inches of sawdust on the floor to keep the space clean and quiet. In these early hours the kitchen had a very serene calm and a particular odor, not yet of food, but somehow a clean, warm, embracing smell.

My first job of the day was to light the coal stove and stoke the fires. Putting coal into the fires was something that I would do many times over the course of the day. Once they got going, all of the coal stoves made the kitchen hot, really, really hot. Our part of the kitchen was particularly hot because the sauce station was between the *rôtisseur* and the *entremetier*, where all the hot garnishes and side dishes were sent. Our station was a massive stove with a flat cook top and an oven. Because the stoves were coal, there were no burners. So if we needed a flame for quick hot cooking, we would remove the rings from the stovetop to cook directly over the flames. We would control the oven temperature by opening and closing the oven doors; in most cases we would prop them open with plates. We also had a counter to work on, but there was no icebox. When an order required something cold, somebody from the *garde-manger* would run it over to us.

My *mise-en-place* duty of the morning determined my mood. If it was something like preparing the Bouillabaisse (see page 125), I was joyful because I loved this dish and the meticulous way that each fish had its own flavor: the cockles and mussels were flavored with saffron, the rascasse with fennel, and the rouget with leeks. If I didn't know the recipe or technique required by heart, I would be filled with apprehension that my lack of skill would slow me down and the chef would call after me to hurry *"vas-y petit!"*

I would speed through the kitchen collecting all of the essential ingredients from the different stations—vegetables from the garde-manger, fish from the icebox, and meat and bones from the butcher—and return them to our counter so Lejay could begin to work. After enough time passed and it seemed that I proved to be a good enough pupil, Chef would let me start the sauces, the Bisque d'Ecrevisses or the Sauce Américaine, by myself. This was always a big day for me.

At 10 o'clock in the morning a steward would come around with a cart filled with ice and lemonade and beer. He would stop and give each person a liter of cheap beer. I liked to combine the lemonade and beer and keep it cold in a bain-marie filled with ice. We would all try to keep our cold drinks going throughout the morning to keep cool and to keep from dehydrating. Every now and then Lejay would yell *"Moule petit! Moule!"* and that would be my order to refill his glass.

The staff was very big, with more than sixty cooks and maybe one hundred waiters in the restaurant. The kitchen was so immense that there were parts of it I never got to see. The rules of the kitchen were still the old, strict style of the brigade, where everyone had a defined place in the ranks that commanded respect. In actuality, what it really meant was that a *commis* rarely talked and never ever contradicted, questioned the authority of, or argued with the chefs, *sous chefs,* or *chefs de partie.* It also meant that moving up through the ranks was very difficult. Once you reached the position of *chef de partie*, you almost always stayed there. Lejay had been the *chef saucier* for years and would continue on for many more. It would never occur to anyone to move him to a different post for variety or a change of

pace. Back in those days, your post was your career, unless you had the talent and the drive to become a head chef.

Within the ranks, there was a post called *la commune*. The holder of this job had the responsibility of cooking for the staff. We ate twice a day, once before lunch service and once before dinner. The food was solid and nourishing: pork chops, roast chicken, and mashed potatoes were often on the menu. Folding tables were set up in the garde-manger in the shape of a T. The chefs all sat along the top of the T and all the commis and cooks down the length. Only the chefs were allowed to drink wine at meals; the rest of us had beer, except for me. Lejay didn't like wine, he only drank beer. I always sat as close to him as I could at the intersection of the tables, so he could pass me his glass of wine while we were eating.

In the restaurant, the style of service was classic French. The chef would call the orders and Lejay would answer. We would immediately start to finish the sauces, which were usually served in silver sauceboats on the side. We would line up the filled boats at our pass on the edge of the stove for the pick-up. The waiters would go from station to station to collect all of the components of their order. If a plate needed to be sauced before it was presented at the table, Lejay would carry the sauce to the pass at another station and sauce the plate before it went out to the dining room.

When the head chef tried to rotate the staff to different posts in the kitchen, I spent one week at the garde-manger. I did not like this station at all because the dishes were cold appetizers and salads that I did not find very interesting. The garde-manger was also located directly in front of Chef Buffeteau's office, which made it the least popular place in the kitchen because the chef could always keep an eye on your work. This was very intimidating because his sense of discipline was extreme and he never complimented the young cooks. I did not do a very good job at this post, as I was quite uncomfortable and the ambiance was so different from my comfortable, student-teacher relationship with Lejay. Plus, everyone tried too hard to impress the chef and this created a very unhealthy competition. After I had spent one unsuccessful week in the garde-manger, the chef gave up and sent me back to Lejay. I was never again transferred.

Lejay and I worked together, side by side, almost every day for more than two years. At first I had been quite afraid of him because I didn't know what to expect. But we soon worked very well together and became partners. I would always try to take the work from his hands to finish it myself. He, being a great teacher, allowed me to stretch myself.

French citizenship of the time required every young person to spend two years in the army. In 1965, I left my sauce stove to serve my country as a paratrooper. Shortly after I left I got a letter from Georges Buffeteau, who had always taken a special interest in me because he knew my father. His letter was full of advice. He told me to "enjoy your time away from this business and fill your lungs with fresh air because once you return it will be a long, long life working hard." He was so right!

I went back to Café de la Paix in the spring of 1973. I was wooing Mary Dunn (who eventually became my wife) with a month-long trip to France. We spent the first week in Paris and I took her to see the restaurant where I had my first job. We entered through the same stairway that I had taken so many times. (I don't think I have ever entered the restaurant through the front doors.) The kitchen still had sawdust on the floor and was almost the same except for some new equipment. And Charles Lejay was still there. He remembered me because I had written to him over the years, letting him know where I was working and how I was doing. He seemed very pleased to see me. I introduced him to my American girlfriend and felt that he acknowledged that I had done well. That was the last time I saw him. My life started to change, I got busy, I moved to New York, and I stopped writing. These are all probably just excuses—I think there was a part of me that just didn't want to witness the end of his career at the Café.

Of all the people I have worked for, I cherish most the memories of working for Charles Lejay. He was never a teacher who was easy to please and I never succeeded in becoming his equal. He was not a famous chef, but I knew that through all my professional life I would respect and keep the foundations that he had taught me. Beyond the culinary foundation he gave me, Charles Lejay taught me about personal discipline, how to show respect for my colleagues, and to know that, in the hierarchy of the traditional kitchen, there were boundaries and borders that could not be crossed. These are the memories that inspire my cooking. Some people think I put versions of classic dishes on my menu to revive old favorites, which is only half of the truth. What they don't know is that the old French classic isn't the recipe, it's the foundation that Charles Lejay instilled in me.

Bisque de Homard
LOBSTER BISQUE

Les Pommes Soufflés
SOUFFLE POTATOES

Deux Gratins Dauphinois
TWO STYLES OF SCALLOPED POTATOES

Soufflé d'Epinard
SPINACH SOUFFLE

Quenelles de Brochet
PIKE DUMPLINGS WITH CRAYFISH SAUCE

La Bouillabaisse
FISH STEW

Sole Meunière
SAUTÉED SOLE

Fricassée de Volaille à la Crème à l'Estragon
STEWED CHICKEN WITH CREAM AND TARRAGON

Salmis de Canard
DUCK WITH RED WINE AND FOIE GRAS

Lapin à la Moutarde
ROASTED RABBIT WITH MUSTARD

Gibelotte de Lapin
RABBIT STEW WITH TOMATO AND MUSHROOMS

Selle de Chevreuil Grand Veneur
ROASTED VENISON WITH GRAND VENEUR SAUCE

Civet de Sanglier
WILD BOAR STEW

Aiguillette de Boeuf
BEEF BRAISED IN RED WINE

Carbonnade de Boeuf Flamande
BEEF BRAISED WITH BEER AND ONIONS

Tarte Tatin
UPSIDE-DOWN APPLE TART

Bisque de homard

LOBSTER BISQUE

Traditionally, the lobster is cooked with a Light Fish Stock and then the cream is added at the very end. In my version, I think the soup has more body and more lobster flavor because I use a light Bouillon de Poule (see page 282) and water as the base. I also add the cream just after reducing so that it can take on more of the lobster flavor. The addition of the cream means that you can make this only one day ahead. When ready to serve, remove the soup from the refrigerator and let it sit at room temperature for 10 minutes. Transfer to a nonstick saucepan and gently warm over medium heat, stirring occasionally to make sure that it does not boil; then add the cream. When using the lobster coral, it is sometimes necessary to add only a small amount as it can often impart a very strong flavor into the soup. The cognac will smooth out the rich lobster taste to make a lovely marriage of flavors.

¼ tablespoon coarse salt plus more to taste

Two 2½-pound lobsters

2 tablespoons light olive oil

Freshly ground pepper to taste

6 shallots, peeled and chopped

2 leeks, white part only, well washed and minced

½ cup minced carrots

1 tablespoon tomato paste

¾ cup Armagnac or Cognac

½ cup dry white wine

2 cups Bouillon de Poule (see page 282)

2½ cups heavy cream

3 medium tomatoes, peeled, cored, seeded, and cut into ¼-inch dice

2 large cloves garlic, peeled and crushed

2 sprigs fresh tarragon

1 Bouquet Garni (see page 293)

½ bulb fennel, sliced

1   Fill a large pot with water and add ¼ tablespoon of salt. Place over high heat and bring to a boil. Plunge the lobsters into the boiling water for 2 minutes; then immediately remove them.

2   Cut the lobsters in half, separating the bodies from the tails by twisting them apart. Quarter the tails, lengthwise, smash and remove the claw meat, and discard the sac behind the head. Break the lobsters apart over a mixing bowl so that you can save as much of the juice as possible. When breaking down the tails, there may be a bright red vein of eggs or coral. If so, remove and reserve this with the juice.

3   Heat the oil in a large creuset-style saucepan over high heat. Add the lobster tails and claws, season with salt and pepper to taste and cook for 5 minutes or until the shell turns bright red. Add the shallots, leeks, and carrots and continue to sauté for 5 minutes or until the vegetables are just tender. Stir in the tomato paste and continue to cook, stirring gently, for 3 minutes. Flambé with ½ cup Armagnac. Add the white wine and, stirring constantly, deglaze the pan. Simmer for 5 minutes or until the liquid is reduced by half. Add the Bouillon de Poule and bring to a simmer. Simmer for 3 minutes; then add the cream. The liquid should now cover the lobster and vegetables by about 1 inch. Add the tomatoes, garlic, tarragon, Bouquet Garni, and fennel bulb. Reduce the heat to medium and simmer for 30 minutes.

4   Combine the reserved lobster juice and coral, if any, with the remaining ¼ cup Armagnac. Set aside.

5   Remove the bisque from the heat and pass it through a food mill. Most of the shell should be crushed. If you do not have a food mill, use a mortar and pestle or a wooden rolling pin or a mallet, working it like a large mortar and pestle, to crush the shells in the pot. Return the bisque to the saucepan over medium heat. Add the reserved coral-Armagnac mixture and bring to a boil. Remove from the heat and pass through a coarse sieve. Taste and, if necessary, season with additional salt.

SERVING SUGGESTIONS   Sautéed chanterelle mushrooms, a medallion of cooked lobster or some fresh black truffles shaved over the top would make an excellent garnish.

Les pommes soufflés

SOUFFLE POTATOES

⬤ 1 POTATO PER PERSON

This is more of a technique or process than an actual recipe, although if you follow the guidelines the potatoes will be perfect every time. The key to this method is the double-frying process and the shape. The first fry poaches and cooks the potatoes. The second fry soufflés them and makes them crispy. A double-fry is essential for any deep-fried potato recipe and can be used for French fries as well. For French fries use the same method; just cut the potatoes into sticks.

I really like potatoes, so I usually allow about 1 potato per person. Idaho potatoes are best suited for the soufflés because they have less moisture and more starch. Choose large potatoes that are very hard, an indication that they are young and fresh. Soft potatoes are older and will not crisp as nicely. Do not wash the potatoes after peeling, as this will add water and make them soggy. Instead, wipe them dry with a paper towel. The temperatures of the two frying oils should be checked constantly with an instant-read thermometer to make sure that they are correct. If you plan on making the pommes soufflés often, you might want to invest in a candy thermometer that can be suspended from the side of the pan so that you always know the temperature of the oil.

Canola oil

Idaho potatoes

Coarse salt to taste

Tarte aux pommes bonne Maman PAGE 56

Crème mulligatawny

PAGE 70

Navarin d'agneau printanier PAGE 91

Asperges et morilles
PAGE 181

La bouillabaisse
PAGE 125

Bisque de homard PAGE 114

1   Heat 5 inches of oil in each of two 4-quart saucepans over medium-high heat, one to 300°F and the other to 375°F.

2   Peel the potatoes and wipe them dry with a paper towel. Trim the four sides lengthwise so that each side is flat. Using a mandolin, cut the potatoes into even ⅛-inch-thick slices.

3   Place one or two potato slices into the 300°F oil to make sure the oil will not boil over. Working with a few slices at a time, plunge the potatoes into the 300°F oil, making sure that the pan is not crowded and that the potatoes do not touch one another. Gently stir the potatoes so that they do not stick together while poaching. Poach for about 10 minutes or until they are knife tender.

4   Using a slotted spoon, remove the potatoes from the first oil and, one by one, immediately transfer them into the hotter (375°F) oil. They should puff up immediately and turn golden brown in 2 to 3 seconds. Using a slotted spoon, carefully lift the potatoes from the oil and place on paper towels to drain. Continue frying and checking the oil temperature until all the potatoes are fried. Season with salt to taste and serve immediately.

NOTE   To make Pommes Soufflés in advance, when you take them out of the first oil, lay them side by side on a baking sheet lined with a kitchen towel, taking care that they do not touch. Cover and store in a cool place for 1 day or freeze for 4 to 5 days. When ready to serve, follow directions from Step 4.

Deux gratins dauphinois

TWO STYLES OF SCALLOPED POTATOES

SERVES 4

One recipe is made with cream and the other with custard. Although I prefer the cream, both are delicious! The one with cream is more rustic and cheesy and goes well with roasted meats like leg of lamb or roast. The custard gratin is more subtle and sophisticated. It goes well with poultry, rabbit, veal, or even fish. This dish has been served in homes and restaurants throughout France for generations.

1 clove garlic, peeled and crushed

5 tablespoons unsalted butter

1¾ cups of whole milk

¼ cup crème fraîche

3 large eggs, beaten

Pinch freshly ground nutmeg

Coarse salt to taste

Freshly ground pepper to taste

2 pounds Yukon Gold potatoes, peeled, washed, dried, and cut crosswise into ⅛-inch-thick slices

1   Preheat the oven to 375°F.

2   Rub the inside of a 9-inch by 12-inch by 2½-inch baking dish with the clove of garlic. When the dish is well seasoned, discard the garlic. Using 1 tablespoon of the butter, lightly coat the inside of the garlic-scented baking dish. Set aside.

3   Place the milk in a medium saucepan over medium heat and bring to a boil.

4   Combine the crème fraîche and eggs in a mixing bowl. Whisking constantly, add the hot milk and nutmeg. Season with salt and pepper to taste.

5   Layer the potatoes evenly over the bottom of the prepared dish, slightly overlapping the edges. Continue making layers until all of the potato slices have been used. Pour

the milk mixture over the potatoes and season to taste with salt, pepper, and, if desired, additional nutmeg.

6   Cut the remaining butter into small pieces and place over the top of the potatoes.

7   Place in the preheated oven and bake for 5 minutes. Reduce the heat to 325°F and bake for an additional 45 minutes or until a knife inserted into the potatoes comes out clean. Serve immediately.

5 tablespoons unsalted butter

4 cups heavy cream

Freshly ground nutmeg to taste

Coarse salt to taste

Freshly ground pepper to taste

2 pounds Idaho potatoes, peeled, washed, dried, and sliced crosswise ⅛ inch thick

4 cloves garlic, peeled and crushed

¾ cup grated Gruyere cheese

1   Preheat the oven to 325°F.

2   Using 1 tablespoon of the butter, lightly coat a 9-inch by 12-inch by 2½-inch baking dish. Set aside.

3   Place the cream in a 3-quart saucepan over medium-high heat. Season to taste with nutmeg, salt, and pepper and bring to a boil (you may have to lift the pan from the heat to keep it from boiling over). Immediately lower the heat and simmer for 3 minutes. Add the potatoes and simmer, stirring constantly, for 5 minutes. The cream should be slightly thickened.

4   Melt 1 tablespoon of the remaining butter in a small saucepan over low heat. Add the garlic cloves and cook, stirring frequently, for 5 minutes, making sure that the butter does not brown or burn.

5   Spread half of the potatoes in an even layer over the bottom of the prepared dish. Evenly sprinkle half of the cheese over the potatoes. Repeat using the remaining potatoes and cheese.

6   Cut the remaining 3 tablespoons of butter into small pieces and place over the final cheese layer.

7   Place in the preheated oven and bake for 30 minutes or until a knife inserted into the potatoes comes out clean and the top is bubbling and golden brown. Serve immediately.

Soufflé d'epinard

SPINACH SOUFFLE

● SERVES 4

In the kitchen, most young cooks, myself included, were apprehensive about making soufflés. The older guys in the kitchen would tease the younger ones by shouting "petit va chercher la pompe à soufflé," which, loosely translated, means, "go get the air pump to pump up your soufflé." The kitchen at Café de la Paix was no exception.

This soufflé is delicious. The trick to a perfect soufflé is to make sure there is practically no moisture or water remaining in the spinach. The base of the soufflé is a béchamel sauce that gives it stability under the weight of the spinach. At the Café we only used Gruyère, but I have added some Parmesan to toughen up the soufflé a bit. The cheese gives body to the soufflé and its wonderful flavor adds a little kick to the spinach.

At the Café it was served as a side dish. It is also a perfect dish for a Sunday brunch at home with friends.

4 tablespoons unsalted butter

4 tablespoons all-purpose flour

10 ounces fresh spinach

2 teaspoons light olive oil

Coarse salt to taste

Freshly ground pepper to taste

2 cups, plus 2 tablespoons milk

4 large eggs, separated

3 ounces Gruyere cheese, grated

2 ounces Parmesan cheese, grated

Pinch freshly ground nutmeg

1   Preheat the oven to 375°F.

2   Using 1 tablespoon of butter and 1 tablespoon of flour, lightly coat five 6-ounce soufflé dishes or one 1-quart soufflé dish. Set aside.

3   Fill a large mixing bowl or the kitchen sink with cold water. Put the spinach into the water and gently rub it together. Scoop out and drain the spinach. Drain the water and clean the bowl or sink, making sure all of the sand and dirt are removed. Repeat this process three times, starting with fresh water each time. Even though this is time-consuming, it is important to do this, as there is nothing more unpleasant than biting into gritty spinach. Cut off the stems and pat dry. Reserve the leaves between two paper towels.

4   Heat the oil in a 10- to-13-inch sauté pan over high heat. Add the spinach and quickly sauté for 1 to 2 minutes or until it is wilted and dark green. Transfer the spinach to a colander and press it with the back of a large spoon to drain off all of the excess liquid. When it is very well drained, roughly chop the spinach using a chef's knife. Season with salt and pepper to taste and set aside.

5   Melt the remaining 3 tablespoons of butter in a 2- to 3-quart saucepan over medium heat. Add the remaining 3 tablespoons of flour, stirring constantly to make sure that it does not brown. Cook for 3 to 5 minutes until the roux is smooth and well blended.

6   While the roux is cooking, place 2 cups of the milk in a 2- to 3-quart saucepan over medium heat and bring to a boil. Pour the hot milk in a thin stream into the roux, whisking constantly to avoid any lumps. Cook, stirring constantly, for 10 minutes or until smooth and slightly thick. Remove from the heat and pass through a fine mesh sieve into a clean bowl.

7   Whisk the egg yolks into the remaining 2 tablespoons of cold milk until well blended. Then whisk the yolks into the cooled béchamel, mixing until well blended. Set aside.

8   Combine the reserved spinach and the sauce with the Gruyere, Parmesan, and nutmeg in a large bowl. Season with salt and pepper to taste.

9   Using an electric mixer or whisk, whip the egg whites until stiff peaks form. Set aside.

10 Using a rubber spatula, very gently fold ⅓ of the reserved beaten egg whites into the spinach mixture. Repeat two more times until all of the egg whites are incorporated, taking care not to overmix and deflate them. Pour ½ of the mixture into each of the prepared soufflé dishes. Reduce oven temperature to 325°F and bake for 20 minutes or until the top is golden brown, firm and springs back to the touch. Do not open the oven for the first 10 to 15 minutes of cooking, as the cold air will cause the soufflés to fall. Remove from the oven and serve immediately.

Quenelles de brochet

PIKE DUMPLINGS WITH CRAYFISH SAUCE

SERVES 4

I love this dish because the quenelles have a velvety, fluffy texture. The right proportions of pâte à choux and fish combine to make the quenelles feather light with a very delicate fish flavor.

At the Café, the preparation or mise en place for this was done by the garde-manger; then the quenelles were cooked and finished by the saucier because of the addition of the Nantua Sauce (see page 288). The recipe for the sauce comes from Nantua, a French town located in the Rhone region of the Alps. The sauce was traditionally made with crayfish that come from the many rivers and streams that flow through the town.

6 tablespoons unsalted butter

1 cup milk or water

¼ teaspoon coarse salt

¼ teaspoon freshly ground nutmeg

6 tablespoons all-purpose flour

3 egg yolks

3 whole eggs

2 pounds pike fillets, ground

2 tablespoons of room temperature unsalted butter

3 cups Fish Stock (see page 287) or water

2 cups Nantua Sauce (see page 288)

I   Preheat the oven to 350°F.

2   Using 1 tablespoon of the butter, lightly coat two 8-inch baking dishes. Set aside.

3   Combine the remaining 5 tablespoons of butter with the milk along with half of the salt and nutmeg in a medium saucepan over medium heat. Bring to a boil. Using a wooden spoon, slowly beat in the flour, and, stirring constantly, cook for about 5 minutes or until the mixture begins to pull away from the side of the saucepan. Remove from the heat and immediately add egg yolks, one at a time, beating vigorously until each egg is well incorporated. Transfer the mixture onto a sheet pan and refrigerate. When well chilled, incorporate same amount of "Panade" with the ground pike fillet. When well combined, add the whole eggs, one at a time, the butter, and the remaining salt and nutmeg. When ingredients are well combined, place the bowl into an ice bath.

4   Immediately begin shaping quenelles (see below). Place the finished quenelles in a single layer in one of the prepared baking dishes.

5   Place the Fish Stock (or water) in a small saucepan over high heat and bring to a boil. Pour the boiling liquid over the quenelles and allow to set for 1 minute.

6   Using a slotted spoon, carefully lift the quenelles from the dish and place on a double thickness of paper towels to drain.

7   Place the drained quenelles in a single layer in the remaining prepared baking dish. Cover with Nantua Sauce and place in the preheated oven. Bake for 5 minutes or until heated through and the sauce is bubbling. Serve immediately.

La bouillabaisse

FISH STEW

● SERVES 4 TO 6

This was "un jour de fête" when Chef Lejay would cook la bouille as we called it. I feel very fortunate to have worked with him and to have learned how to properly cook this aromatic fish soup. The smells of saffron, garlic, and the "finest" of fish filled the kitchen with a delicious aroma. The flambé of garlic in olive oil at the end is the sensational finale to a perfect dish.

The secret to this bouillabaisse is the overnight marination of the fish. You can make it and serve it on the same day, but it will not be as flavorful. Since its signature is the intense and robust flavor, try to allow the extra time. There are three additional recipes that go into making this dish: Fond de Bouillabaisse, Croutons, and Rouille. I recommend that you read through all the recipes before you do your shopping and begin cooking. When buying the fish make sure you get the heads and bones of all the fish to use for the fond and please note that you will also need to buy an additional three lobsters to make the fond.

1 pound boneless hake

1 pound boneless red snapper fillets

1 pound boneless black sea bass fillets

1 pound boneless Alaskan rascasse or rockfish fillets

3 leeks, white part only, well washed, dried, and cut into julienne

2½ medium carrots, peeled, trimmed, and cut into julienne

1 fennel bulb, well washed, dried, and cut into julienne

1 celery heart, well washed, dried, and cut into julienne

4 medium tomatoes, peeled, cored, seeded, and cut in 1-inch cubes

1 head garlic, crushed

¼ cup chopped fresh flat-leaf parsley

2 tablespoons plus 1 teaspoon chopped fresh thyme

2 teaspoons saffron

1½ cups plus 1 tablespoon extra virgin olive oil

¼ cup Ricard

1 tablespoon coarse salt plus more to taste

Three 1-pound lobsters

12 mussels

8 clams

8 sea scallops

1 quart Fond de Bouillabaisse (see recipe below)

1 tablespoon chopped garlic

Croutons (see recipe below)

Rouille (see recipe below)

Freshly ground pepper to taste

1   Keeping each fish separate, cut the hake, snapper, bass, and rascasse fillets into long strips about 1 inch wide.

2   Arrange each fish in a single layer in a large shallow nonreactive baking dish. Put one type of julienned vegetable on top of each fish. (You can combine them as you wish, for example the leeks on top of the red snapper, the carrots on top of the black sea bass, etc.) When the fish and vegetables have been layered, add the tomatoes, crushed garlic head, 2 tablespoons parsley, 2 tablespoons thyme, and 1 teaspoon saffron. Drizzle the 1½ cups olive oil and the Ricard over the vegetables, distributing evenly over all the fish. Cover with plastic film and refrigerate overnight.

3   Fill a 5-quart saucepan with cold water. Add 1 tablespoon of salt, place over high heat, and bring to a boil. Immediately plunge the lobsters into the boiling water and cook for 3 minutes or until they are bright red. Drain well and carefully separate the tails from

the bodies. Remove the claws and reserve them in the shell. Reserve the bodies for the Fond de Bouillabaisse (recipe follows). Cut the tails in half lengthwise, and reserve.

4   Combine the marinated fish and vegetables and all of the marinating liquid with the mussels, clams, and scallops along with ½ teaspoon of the remaining saffron and the remaining 2 tablespoons of parsley and 1 teaspoon of thyme in a large (about 12-quart) creuset-style cast-iron casserole with a cover. Stir in the Fond de Bouillabaisse. Cover and place over high heat. Bring to a boil; then lower the heat and simmer for 10 minutes or until the clams and mussels open. Turn off the heat and remove the lid. Add the lobster tails and claws, cover, and let stand for 2 to 3 minutes. Uncover. Taste and, if necessary, adjust the seasoning with salt and pepper.

5   Heat the remaining 1 tablespoon of olive oil in a small sauté pan over high heat. Add the chopped garlic and sauté for 1 minute. Immediately add the garlic to the bouillabaisse.

6   Place the pot on the table and serve La Bouillabaisse with the croutons and Rouille on the side. As the Rouille is a condiment, it can first be spread on the croutons and then the croutons can be laid on top of the bouillabaisse, or it can be put directly into the bouillabaisse. It is your choice. Add pepper if desired.

Fond de bouillabaisse

BOUILLABAISSE STOCK

MAKES 1 QUART PLUS

To give the fond a very intense flavor, the fish bones are marinated overnight in the refrigerator. You can marinate them for less time, but the flavors will not be as strong. The finished fond can be stored in an airtight container in the refrigerator for 24 hours.

Head and bones of 1 hake

Head and bones of 1 red snapper

Head and bones of 1 black sea bass or striped bass

Head and bones 1 Alaskan rascasse or rockfish

Lobster bodies, claws reserved for another use

3 stalks celery, washed and chopped

2 cups dry white wine

4 medium tomatoes, washed and halved

2 medium onions, peeled and sliced

2 carrots, washed and sliced

2 leeks, white part only, washed and chopped

1 bulb fennel, washed and chopped

1 head garlic, peeled and crushed

2 tablespoons tomato paste

2 tablespoons Ricard

2½ teaspoons saffron

Coarse salt to taste

Freshly ground pepper to taste

1   Combine the fish heads and bones, lobster bodies, and celery. Add the white wine, tomatoes, onions, carrots, leeks, fennel, garlic, tomato paste, Ricard, and saffron in large bowl and cover with plastic film; place in the refrigerator to marinate overnight. (You can also marinate the stock in the same pot in which you are going to cook.)

2   Remove the bowl from the refrigerator and skim off and reserve any excess oil from the surface. Remove the fish heads, bones, and lobster bodies and reserve. Reserve the marinade and the vegetables.

3   Heat the reserved oil in a large saucepan (about 10 inches deep) over low heat. Add the fish heads and bones and sweat for 5 to 10 minutes or until they are soft, taking care that they do not brown. Add the reserved lobster bodies, marinade, and vegetables and, stirring constantly, deglaze the pan. Bring to a simmer and simmer for 5 to 10 minutes or until the liquid is reduced by half.

4   Add enough water to cover everything by 1½ to 2 inches. Bring to a simmer and simmer for 30 minutes, periodically skimming off any foam that forms on the surface. Place the skimmed foam in a bowl and reserve. You will need at least ½ cup of foam for the Rouille (see below).

5   Pass the fond through a food mill; then strain it through a mesh sieve into a clean saucepan. Place over medium heat and bring to a boil. Lower the heat and simmer for 5 minutes. Season with salt and pepper to taste. Transfer to a nonreactive bowl. Cover with plastic film and store in the refrigerator for up to 24 hours.

Rouille

SERVES 4

Rouille is the traditional condiment that accompanies bouillabaisse. It literally means rusty, which is a good description of its color. Rouille can be spread on bread or croutons and dunked into the soup. It can also be spooned directly into the broth; as it melts it will thicken the stew and add smoothness along with another layer of flavor and texture. The egg yolks carry the flavor and add an extra richness to the rouille. Do not worry about using raw egg yolks, as there is enough heat from the baked potato to cook them.

1 Idaho potato, washed

2 large egg yolks

5 cloves garlic, peeled and mashed

1 cup extra-virgin olive oil

Coarse salt to taste

½ cup Fond de Bouillabaisse foam (see above)

1   Preheat the oven to 375°F.

2   Randomly pierce the potato with a fork and place on a baking sheet in the preheated oven. Bake for 40 minutes or until a knifepoint is easily inserted into the center. Immediately cut the potato in half lengthwise and scoop out all the flesh, discarding the skin.

3   Combine the potato flesh and egg yolks with the garlic and olive oil in a small mixing bowl. Season with salt to taste and beat until well blended. Beating constantly, gradually add the Fond de Bouillabaisse foam. The Rouille should be slightly thick and not too runny. Use as directed in the specific recipe.

Croutons

Make these only a few hours ahead, as they should be prepared and eaten in the same day. Croutons are a part of the traditional bouillabaisse service but they also make a nice addition to any soup or salad.

1 cup olive oil

One 1½-pound loaf country bread, cut crosswise into ¾-inch-thick slices

2 cloves garlic, peeled and crushed

Heat the oil in a large sauté pan over medium heat. Add the bread slices a few at a time and fry, turning occasionally, for about 2 minutes or until golden brown on all sides. Remove from the pan and drain on paper towels. When they are well drained, rub both sides of each slice of bread with garlic. Serve warm or at room temperature.

Sole meunière

SAUTÉED SOLE

•	SERVES 4

In France, this is one of the most popular sole preparations, so much so that Proust himself described it in one of his novels. Although it is simple, I think that it is the best way to cook a whole fish. The dish is served with a beurre noisette, which is butter cooked until it is foamy and a nutty brown color. The richness of the butter is cut with fresh lemon juice. Since this is the most fundamental recipe for preparing fish, you can truly cook almost any fish in this fashion. In fact, I think that there is not a fish that doesn't taste superb as meunière.

3 tablespoons all-purpose flour

4 whole 1-pound sole, head, fins, and gray skin removed, white skin scraped or removed

Coarse salt to taste

Freshly ground pepper to taste

¼ cup clarified butter (see page 290)

7 tablespoons unsalted butter

2 tablespoons chopped fresh flat-leaf parsley

Juice of 1 lemon

1   Preheat the oven to 350°F.

2   Place the flour in a wide shallow plate.

3   Season the sole on both sides with salt and pepper; then lightly dredge in the flour, making sure that the fish is lightly coated on both sides. Shake off any excess flour.

4   Heat the clarified butter in an oval frying pan made especially for fish over medium-high heat. Add one sole, white skin down, and sauté for 5 minutes or until it is golden brown. Using a fish spatula, flip the fish and cook for another 5 minutes or until it is

golden brown. Using the spatula, transfer the fish to a baking sheet. Repeat with the remaining 3 fish.

5   Place the fried fish in the preheated oven and bake for 3 minutes or until the flesh starts to separate and pull away from the bone. Remove from the oven and, using the spatula, carefully transfer the fish to a serving platter.

6   Place the butter in a small frying pan over medium heat. After about 3 minutes, it will start to foam and turn a light golden brown in color. Watch carefully as this happens very quickly. Remove from the heat.

7   Sprinkle the sole with parsley and a pinch of salt. Drizzle lemon juice over the fish, and then pour the *beurre noisette* over the top. Serve immediately.

Fricassée de volaille à

STEWED CHICKEN WITH CREAM AND TARRAGON

la crème l'estragon

SERVES 4

This classic dish is similar to Blanquette de Veau (see page 94) in taste and texture. The main difference is that the chicken is sautéed instead of being poached. Today this wonderful dish is hard to find on menus, as people have become more concerned with fat and calories than with flavor and tradition.

One 4- to 5-pound chicken, quartered

Coarse salt to taste

Freshly ground pepper to taste

2 tablespoons light olive oil

7 tablespoons unsalted butter

3 shallots, peeled and chopped

1½ medium onions, peeled and cut into ¼-inch dice

1 cup dry white wine

6 cups White Veal Stock (see page 285)

3 sprigs fresh tarragon

1 teaspoon dried tarragon

3 tablespoons all-purpose flour

1 cup heavy cream

2 large egg yolks

2 tablespoons crème fraîche

1 teaspoon fresh lemon juice

1 tablespoon fresh tarragon leaves, blanched and chopped

1   Generously season the chicken on all sides with salt and pepper to taste.

2   Heat the olive oil in a large heavy-duty skillet over medium heat. Add the chicken and sear, turning occasionally, for 3 to 5 minutes or until golden brown on all sides. Transfer to paper towels to drain. Pat dry and reserve.

3   Melt 3 tablespoons of the butter in a large saucepan over low heat. Add the shallots and onions and sweat for 3 minutes, taking care that they do not brown. Add the reserved chicken and then the wine. Raise the heat and bring to a simmer. Immediately, lower the heat and gently simmer for 5 to 10 minutes or until the liquid is reduced by half. Add the White Veal Stock (which should cover the chicken by ½ inch). Again, raise the heat and bring to a boil. Stir in the fresh tarragon sprigs along with the dried tarragon. Lower the heat and simmer for 20 minutes. (Check the chicken breasts from time to time. They should just feel tender to the touch, but it is important not to overcook the chicken. In fact, it is okay if it is a bit undercooked at this point.) Using a slotted spoon, remove the chicken breasts and reserve them in a bowl with a damp cloth placed over the top. Keep warm on the back of the stove.

4   Cook the legs for an additional 10 minutes. Using a slotted spoon, remove the legs and reserve them with the breasts.

5   Continue to simmer the liquid for 10 minutes or until it is reduced by one quarter. The broth should have an equal flavor balance between the chicken and the tarragon.

6   Melt the remaining 4 tablespoons of butter in a small saucepan over medium heat. Blend in the flour, whisking until a smooth paste forms. Cook, stirring constantly, for 3 minutes, taking care that the roux does not brown. Remove from the heat and allow to cool to room temperature.

7   Whisk the reduced sauce into the cooled roux. Place over medium-low heat and bring to a simmer. Simmer for 5 to 8 minutes or until reduced by one third. Pass the sauce through a fine mesh sieve and reserve.

8   Remove and discard the rib bones from the breasts. Combine the deboned breasts with the remaining reserved chicken and the sauce in a large saucepan over medium heat. Bring to a boil; then add the heavy cream. Lower the heat and simmer, stirring frequently, for 5 minutes.

9   Beat the egg yolks, crème fraîche, and lemon juice until smooth. Remove the chicken from the heat and gently stir the yolk mixture into the sauce. Add the blanched tarragon and season with salt and pepper to taste.

Salmis de canard

DUCK WITH RED WINE AND FOIE GRAS

SERVES 4

The duck is marinated and braised in red wine like a Bœuf Bourguignon, but the sauce makes a more defined statement, as it is enriched by the foie gras. This is a perfect combination of classic French cooking and the cuisine de terroir of southwest France, because of the use of foie gras and moulard duck, both local Gascon products. The contemporary version of this dish is to serve a rich sauce with Magret duck that has been simply grilled to rare or, at the most, medium-rare. The same style dish is also done using either pheasant or squab.

When purchasing the duck, check for fat, as you will need 3 tablespoons to complete the recipe. If the fat has been removed or is skimpy, you will have to purchase additional duck fat to create the desired flavor for the finished dish.

The duck legs marinate for 2 days in the refrigerator. This allows the seasonings to really mesh together and to permeate the meat. You can shorten the marinade time to a few hours, but the end result simply will not be as succulent.

8 whole Moulard duck legs

3½ cups red wine

1 medium carrot, peeled and halved lengthwise

½ medium onion, peeled and sliced

½ head garlic, peeled and chopped

1 tablespoon olive oil

1 teaspoon tomato paste

1 sprig fresh flat-leaf parsley

1 sprig fresh thyme

½ bay fresh leaf

1 teaspoon freshly ground pepper plus more to taste

¼ teaspoon coarse salt plus more to taste

3 tablespoons duck fat (see instructions)

2 medium onions, peeled and cut into ¼-inch dice

1½ tablespoons all-purpose flour

3 cups Duck Jus (see page 287)

¼ pound mushrooms, white button, small chanterelles, or cèpes, cleaned, stems removed, and chopped

¼ pound pearl onions, peeled and blanched

3 tablespoons unsalted butter

2 tablespoons water

1 teaspoon sugar

½ pound slab bacon, blanched and cut into ½-inch strips

2 tablespoons Foie Gras Butter (see recipe below)

1. Inspect each leg to locate any fat, which is under the skin at each end of the leg and by the joint in the middle. The fat is white and looks a little like wax. To remove it, simply pull it out with your fingers or cut it out with a paring knife. You should have about 3 tablespoonfuls. Wrap it in plastic wrap and refrigerate for later use.

2. Place the duck legs in a single layer in a shallow 3-quart dish. Combine 2 cups of the red wine with the carrot, sliced onion, garlic, olive oil, tomato paste, parsley, thyme, and bay leaf, along with 1 teaspoon of the pepper and ¼ teaspoon of the salt. Pour the red wine marinade over the legs. Wrap the entire dish with plastic film and place in the refrigerator to marinate for 2 days.

3. When ready to cook the duck, preheat the oven to 350°F.

4. Remove the duck legs from the marinade, separately reserving the marinade. Season the legs with salt and pepper to taste on all sides.

5 Heat 1 tablespoon of duck fat over medium heat in a large creuset-style pan with a lid. Cook for 2 minutes or until it is melted. Add the duck legs and sear for 5 minutes or until golden brown on all sides. Remove and allow to drain on paper towels. Pat dry and reserve.

6 Add another tablespoon of duck fat and cook over medium heat for 2 minutes or until melted. Add the chopped onions and reserved duck legs and sweat for 5 minutes, taking care that the onions do not brown. Stir in the flour and cook, stirring constantly, for 5 minutes, taking care that the mixture does not brown. Add the remaining 1½ cups red wine and stir to deglaze the pan. Bring to a boil. Lower the heat and simmer for 15 minutes or until the liquid is reduced by half. Add the Duck Jus and 1 cup of the reserved marinade and bring to a boil. Cover the cooking surface with a piece of parchment paper cut into a circle to exactly fit the inside of the pan. Cover with the lid and place in the preheated oven. Cook for 1 hour or until the duck legs are knife tender.

7 Remove the saucepan from the oven and reduce the oven temperature to 180°F. Using a slotted spoon, carefully remove the duck legs from the sauce and place on a serving platter. Cover with a damp kitchen towel and reserve in a warm spot (the back of the stove works well). Do not turn off the oven.

8 Place the saucepan over high heat and bring the sauce to a boil. Lower the heat slightly and boil for 5 minutes, occasionally skimming any oil or scum that rises to the surface. Again, lower the heat and simmer for 8 minutes or until the liquid has reduced by half. Remove from the heat and pass the sauce through a fine mesh sieve, discarding the solids. Set aside.

9 Melt the remaining 1 tablespoon of duck fat in a medium sauté pan over medium heat. Add the mushrooms and sauté for 5 minutes or until golden brown. Drain off and discard any liquid. Season with salt and pepper to taste and set aside.

10 Combine the pearl onions, butter, water, and sugar in a medium sauté pan over medium heat. Cook, stirring occasionally, for 5 minutes or until nicely glazed and golden brown. Set aside.

11 Place the bacon in a medium sauté pan over medium heat and fry for 5 minutes or until golden brown and slightly crisp. Drain on paper towels and reserve.

12 Place the duck legs in a single layer on an ovenproof serving platter and place them in the preheated oven for 5 minutes.

13 Place the reserved sauce in a medium saucepan over medium-high heat and bring to a boil. Immediately remove from the heat and beat in the Foie Gras Butter, whisking until

well blended. Strain through a fine mesh sieve into a clean saucepan. Place over very low heat to keep warm. Taste, and if necessary, adjust the seasoning with salt and pepper.

14   Remove the legs from the oven. If any juice has accumulated on the platter, whisk it into the warm sauce. Pour the sauce over the legs; then evenly distribute the reserved mushrooms, bacon, and pearl onions over the top.

Foie gras butter

MAKES ½ CUP

This can be made 1 day in advance and stored in an airtight container in the refrigerator.

4 ounces fresh grade B foie gras, or trimmings of foie gras from another recipe

4 tablespoons unsalted butter, at room temperature

1   Place the foie gras in a small sauté pan over high heat. Sauté, turning frequently, for 3 to 5 minutes or until it is golden brown. Using a slotted spoon, lift the foie gras to paper towels to drain. When it is well drained, transfer to a plate. Place in the refrigerator to chill for 20 minutes.

2   Combine the chilled foie gras and butter in a small mixing bowl. Using a wooden spoon (or a food processor fitted with the metal blade), beat (or process) until smooth and creamy. Transfer to an airtight container (or to a bowl covered tightly with plastic wrap) and store, refrigerated, for up to 1 day.

Lapin à la moutarde

ROASTED RABBIT WITH MUSTARD

> ● SERVES 4

An occasional spring special on the menu at Café de la Paix, this dish was carved tableside in the dining room and served with its own juice. It is very simple and easy to do. You will probably have to go to a specialty market or butcher to find fresh rabbit. So you might as well have the rabbit trimmed and prepared by the butcher. The rabbit is marinated in mustard for a day to keep it moist during cooking and to really impart the tangy mustard flavor required in the finished dish.

One 3½-pound rabbit

1 cup Dijon mustard

1 tablespoon olive oil

2 tablespoons water

¾ cup Rabbit Jus (see page 287)

Coarse salt to taste

Freshly ground pepper to taste

1   Place the rabbit in a heavy shallow roasting pan big enough to comfortably hold the rabbit but small enough to fit in your refrigerator. Spread the mustard evenly over the rabbit. Completely wrap the roasting pan with plastic film and place in the refrigerator for at least 8 hours or up to 24 hours.

2   Preheat the oven to 350°F.

3   Remove the rabbit from the refrigerator, unwrap, and let it rest on the counter for 15 to 20 minutes or until it has reached room temperature.

4   Dip a pastry brush into the olive oil and shake it over the rabbit to sprinkle it with the oil. Place the rabbit in the preheated oven and immediately turn the temperature up to 425°F. Roast for 10 minutes; then reduce the temperature to 370°F and roast for an additional 15 minutes. Finally, reduce the temperature to 350°F and roast for another 15 to 20 minutes. Remove the rabbit from the oven. Cover loosely with aluminum foil and let rest for 10 minutes.

5   Remove the rabbit from the roasting pan and place it on a serving platter.

6   Place the roasting pan over low heat. Add the water and, stirring constantly, deglaze the pan, scraping the bottom of the pan to release all the brown bits. Stir in the Rabbit Jus, raise the heat, and bring to a boil. Immediately, lower the heat and simmer for 5 minutes. Remove from the heat and strain through a fine mesh sieve into a clean bowl. Taste and adjust the seasoning with salt and pepper. Pour the sauce over the rabbit and serve.

Gibelotte de lapin

RABBIT STEW WITH TOMATO AND MUSHROOMS

SERVES 4

Originally the dish was made with game birds and then somehow evolved to be a rabbit dish. In colloquial French the gibelotte is the pouch a hunter carries. The idea is that as the hunter is walking through the forest, he will pick up mushrooms and herbs along the way to cook with his game.

2 sprigs fresh thyme

2 sprigs fresh tarragon

4 cloves garlic, peeled

One 3-pound rabbit, cut into 5 pieces: 4 legs and the center loin

2 tablespoons light olive oil

Coarse salt to taste

Freshly ground pepper to taste

6 cloves garlic, unpeeled

1½ cups dry white wine

3 medium tomatoes, peeled, cored, seeded, and crushed

2 medium onions, peeled and cut into ¼-inch dice

1 teaspoon tomato paste

1 bay leaf

2 cups Rabbit Jus (see page 287)

4 tablespoons olive oil

4 cooked small Yukon gold potatoes (about 2½ inches long by 1 inch in diameter)
    with skin on, quartered

½ cup chanterelles or other wild mushroom, cleaned and sliced

2 tablespoons chopped shallots

1 teaspoon chopped garlic

1 tablespoon chopped fresh flat leaf parsley

1 teaspoon fresh thyme leaves

2 cups tiny dandelion greens or baby arugula, well washed and dried

1   Place one sprig each of thyme and tarragon along with the 4 peeled cloves of garlic in the cavity of the rabbit loin. Tie the loin closed with 3 rings of string with the fluffs closed around it. Place in a shallow dish, wrap tightly with plastic film and refrigerate for 24 hours. Separately wrap and refrigerate the legs.

2   Heat the light olive oil in a large heavy-duty sauté pan over high heat until it is very hot but not smoking. Add the loin and rabbit legs and sear, turning frequently, for about 7 minutes or until golden brown on all sides. Season with salt and pepper to taste. Keeping the rabbit in the pan drain off all but 1 tablespoon of the fat. Add the remaining tarragon and thyme sprigs along with the 6 unpeeled cloves of garlic. Sweat for about 5 minutes, taking care that the garlic does not take on any color. Stir in the wine and cook for about 15 minutes or until the liquid is reduced by half. Stir in the tomatoes, onions, tomato paste, bay leaf, and Rabbit Jus and bring to a boil. Taste the cooking liquid and if it seems too strongly flavored, add up to ¼ cup of water. Lower the heat and simmer for about 10 minutes or until the rabbit loin is fork tender. Using a slotted spoon, remove the loin from the sauce and reserve. Cook the legs for an additional 7 minutes or until they are fork tender. Remove from the heat. Lift the legs from the sauce and reserve with the loin, tenting lightly with aluminium foil to keep warm.

3   Strain the sauce through a fine mesh sieve into a clean saucepan. Place over low heat to just keep hot. Taste and, if necessary, adjust the seasoning with salt and pepper.

4   Heat 3 tablespoons of the olive oil in a large skillet over medium heat. Add the potatoes and season with salt and pepper to taste. Sauté for about 4 minutes or until lightly colored. Add the mushrooms, shallots, and chopped garlic and sauté for an additional 4 minutes, taking care that the garlic and the shallots do not take on any color. Stir in the parsley and thyme leaves and sauté for 1 minute.

5   Combine the remaining 1 tablespoon of olive oil with the greens in a medium sauté pan over medium heat. Season with salt and pepper to taste and sauté for about 3 minutes or until just wilted.

6   Place the rabbit on a serving dish, pour the sauce on top, and evenly distribute the vegetables over the top. Serve immediately.

Selle de chevreuil

ROASTED VENISON WITH GRAND VENEUR SAUCE

grand veneur

● SERVES 4 TO 6

This dish shows the artistry of the saucier by first roasting, then braising, and finally using all the cooking liquids to finish the sauce. This is haute cuisine par excellence and a celebration of the season of game. The type of venison you use will determine the marinating time. Red venison can be marinated for up to 2 hours depending upon the age and the part of the animal used. For a very young animal, say one less than 2 years old, and for smaller breeds such as Roe deer, I do not marinate because the meat is already very tender and mildly flavored. In this instance, I will simply sauté the meat.

The sauce does take a bit of time, since you really have to prepare two sauces—the first sauce is the base for the final one. Read through the recipe with care as you will need to reserve some of the trimmings and some of the marinade for the sauces. For an extra layer of flavor, I like to add the meat juices to the sauce after I have sliced the venison. The peppercorns in the Sauce Poivrade should be sufficient to flavor the end sauce, so season very carefully.

½ cup light olive oil

1½ heads garlic, crushed and unpeeled

1 medium onion, peeled and sliced

1 carrot, peeled and sliced

10 cups dry white wine

1 cup cognac

1 sprig fresh thyme

1 sprig fresh flat-leaf parsley

1 bay leaf

One 4- to 5-pound venison rack and saddle, deboned, trimmings reserved

6 tablespoons olive oil

Coarse salt to taste

2 tablespoons unsalted butter

Sauce Grand Veneur (see recipe below)

1   Heat the light olive oil in a shallow 16-inch by 13-inch braising pan over medium heat. Add the garlic, onion, and carrot, and sweat for 5 minutes or until they are soft, taking care that they do not brown or color. Add the wine, cognac, thyme, parsley, and bay leaf and bring to a boil. Boil for 3 minutes; then lower the heat and simmer for 5 minutes. Remove from the heat and cool.

2   Place the meat into the marinade in the braising pan and tightly cover with plastic film. Place in the refrigerator to marinate for 2 hours.

3   Remove the venison from the refrigerator. Unwrap and remove the meat from the marinade. Cut the meat into 8- to 10-ounce pieces (about 3 inches by 1 inch). Separately reserve 2 cups of the marinade for use in the Sauce Poivrade.

4   Heat the olive oil in a large sauté pan over medium heat for about 3 minutes or until it is smoking hot. Season one side of the meat with salt to taste. Place the meat in the hot oil and sear for about 2 to 3 minutes on each side or until it is a rare to medium-rare temperature and lightly firm to the touch. This is the best internal temperature for venison because it allows all the flavors to come forth with the meat juicy but not too rare, the peak of tenderness. At the moment before you remove the meat from the pan, stir in the butter and baste for 30 seconds to further nourish the meat.

5   Place the meat on a rack set on a serving platter. This will keep the meat from coming into contact with its own juices, which would continue to cook the meat. Cover with a loose piece of parchment paper and allow to rest for 2 minutes. Cut into two pieces each and place on a serving platter. Serve immediately, with the Sauce Grand Veneur on the side.

Sauce grand veneur

● | MAKES 1 QUART |

4 cups Sauce Poivrade (see recipe below)

1 tablespoon unsalted butter

1 to 1½ tablespoons crème fraîche

2 to 2½ teaspoons red currant jelly or jam

1½ teaspoons Armagnac

Coarse salt to taste

Freshly ground pepper to taste

Place the Sauce Poivrade in a medium saucepan over medium heat and bring to a simmer. Remove from the heat and whisk in the butter. When well blended, whisk in the crème fraîche. The sauce should coat the back of a spoon. Whisk in the red currant jelly (to give the sauce a beautiful shine and a hint of tartness). Add the Armagnac. Taste and, if necessary, adjust the seasoning with salt and pepper. Pass the sauce through a fine mesh sieve and reserve.

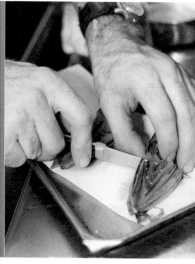

Sauce poivrade

● | MAKES 1½ QUARTS |

2 tablespoons light olive oil or duck fat

2 onions, peeled and cut into ¼-inch dice

2 carrots, peeled, trimmed and cut into ¼-inch dice

1 garlic head, unpeeled, cut in half crosswise

Trimmings from a 4- to 5-pound venison rack

1 cup white wine

4 cups Veal Jus (see page 287)

2 cups venison marinade

10 juniper berries

1 sprig fresh thyme

1 bay leaf

1 tablespoon crushed black peppercorns

1   Heat the olive oil in a braising pan over medium-high heat. Add the onions, carrots, and garlic; sweat, stirring constantly, for about 5 minutes or until the vegetables are soft and an even golden color. Using a slotted spoon, remove the vegetables from the pan and reserve.

2   Add the venison trimmings, a few pieces at a time, to the pan and sear until the trimmings are brown and a nice caramelized film has formed on the bottom of the braising pan.

3   Return the reserved vegetables to the pan and add the wine; stirring constantly, scrape the bottom with a wooden spoon to deglaze the pan and loosen all of the browned bits. Bring to a simmer; then lower the heat and gently simmer for about 8 minutes or until the liquid has reduced by half.

4   Raise the heat and add the Veal Jus. Bring to a boil. Add the venison marinade along with the juniper berries, thyme, and bay leaf. Lower the heat and simmer for about 35 minutes or until the liquid has reduced by half. Every 5 minutes, add 2 tablespoons of cold water to stop the cooking. This process will allow more impurities to come to the surface so that they may be skimmed off. Place the peppercorns in a fine mesh sieve and strain the sauce through them into a clean bowl. Cool to room temperature; then cover and refrigerate until ready to use.

Civet de sanglier

WILD BOAR STEW

> SERVES 6 TO 8

In general, there are two kinds of classic French marinades: raw and cooked. For a big-game meat like this one, you must first cook the marinade and then let it cool so that the flavors have melded together. The meat is then submerged into it. The purpose is to have a well-balanced marinade that will intensify the flavor of the gamy meat. This is a perfect dish for a slightly chilly Sunday in October, especially when served with some poached fruit and Pommes Purée.

10 tablespoons duck fat

2 medium onions, peeled and chopped

2 carrots, peeled, trimmed, and chopped

8 cups red wine (one rich in tannins)

1 head garlic, cut in half crosswise

1 teaspoon freshly ground pepper plus more to taste

2 sprigs fresh flat-leaf parsley

2 sprigs fresh thyme

One 6-pound leg of wild boar, whole shank removed by the butcher

2 cups plus 2 tablespoons Armagnac

3 carrots cut in half lengthwise, blanched

3 medium onions, peeled and sliced

¼ cup all-purpose flour

¼ cup tomato paste

6 cups red wine

1 bay leaf

5 cups Veal Jus (see page 287)

2 cups Bouillon de Poule (see page 282)

Coarse salt to taste

½ cup Foie Gras Butter (see page 139)

1   Heat ¼ cup of the duck fat in a medium saucepan over medium heat. Add the chopped onions and carrots and sweat for about 5 minutes or until the vegetables are soft, taking care that they do not brown or color. Add the tannic red wine and bring the mixture to a boil. Add the garlic and 1 teaspoon pepper along with 1 sprig each of the parsley and thyme. Lower the heat and simmer for 20 minutes. Remove from the heat and allow to come to room temperature.

2   Place the meat in a large glass baking dish. Add the cooled marinade and 2 cups of the Armagnac. Tightly cover with plastic film and refrigerate for 8 days, unwrapping and turning occasionally. After 8 days, remove the boar from the marinade and pat dry. Wrap in plastic film and again refrigerate for 8 hours or overnight. Place the marinade in an airtight container and refrigerate.

3   When ready to roast, preheat the oven to 350°F.

4   Heat the remaining duck fat in a large, deep braising pot with a cover over medium-low heat. Add the blanched carrots and sliced onions and sweat for about 5 minutes or until they are soft, taking care that they do not brown or color. Drain off any excess fat and add the boar leg to the pan. Continue to sweat the leg and the vegetables, giving a light sear to the meat without coloring the vegetables. Stir in the flour and tomato paste and continue to cook for 5 minutes. Raise the heat and add the 6 cups of red wine and the bay leaf. Bring to a boil; then lower the heat and cook for about 45 minutes or until the liquid has reduced by half. Add the Veal Jus and bouillon and again bring to a boil. Lower the heat and bring to a gentle simmer. Cover the surface with a piece of parchment paper cut to fit the inside of the pot. Cover with the lid and place in the preheated oven for about 20 minutes or until the liquid has again reduced by half. Reduce the oven temperature to 325°F

5   Remove the pan from the oven. Uncover and place on the stove top over high heat. Bring to a boil. Immediately, lower the heat to a simmer and cook, frequently skimming the surface of foam, for 10 minutes. Remove the pan from the heat, cover, and return to the preheated oven; cook for 2 to 2½ hours or until the meat is fork tender. Remove from the oven and let rest for 20 minutes.

6   Using a kitchen fork, carefully lift the leg from the cooking liquid and place it on a serving platter. Tent lightly with aluminum foil to keep warm.

7   Strain the braising liquid through a fine mesh sieve into a clean saucepan. Place the braising liquid on the stove top over medium heat and bring to a simmer. Simmer for 10 minutes or until it has reduced by one quarter. Season with salt and pepper to taste. Whisk the Foie Gras Butter and remaining 2 tablespoons of Armagnac into the sauce. Lower the heat to just keep the sauce warm.

8   Cut into the leg lengthwise along the bone, and then slice the meat against the grain into thin serving pieces. Place the sliced meat on a long serving platter and spoon half of the sauce over it. Pass the remaining sauce in a gravy boat.

Aiguillette de boeuf

BEEF BRAISED IN RED WINE

● SERVES 4

This recipe uses bottom round of beef, an inexpensive cut of meat that is usually dismissed as tough and dry. There are three techniques at work that tenderize and flavor the meat: marinating, larding, and braising. You may think a weeklong marinade seems like a lot of trouble, but in fact all you have to do is plan ahead and let the ingredients do the rest. A cut of beef like the bottom round is so lean that it needs to be nourished with additional fat. After the larding, the ratio of meat to fat is no more than that of a nicely marbled piece of steak. The long slow heat of the braising is where all the flavors fuse together. Notice that the final sauce does not require any additional salt or pepper because it is perfectly flavored during the preparation and cooking process.

In the restaurant, this dish was always served with a very simple side dish of egg noodles tossed with butter and chopped parsley. At home, I like to serve it with the somewhat more elegant Fricassee of Cèpe Mushrooms (see page 20) and a Pommes Purée (see page 294).

3 pounds beef bottom round

½ pound pork fatback

1 onion, peeled and chopped

1 carrot, peeled, trimmed, and chopped

1 leek (white part only), washed and chopped

1 head garlic, peeled and chopped

2 sprigs fresh thyme, chopped

2 sprigs fresh flat-leaf parsley, chopped

1 fresh bay leaf, chopped

7 cups red wine

1 tablespoon duck fat or vegetable oil

1½ cups onions chopped into ¼-inch dice

1½ tablespoons tomato paste

1½ tablespoons all-purpose flour

Coarse salt to taste

Freshly ground pepper to taste

½ pound pork rind, blanched

5 cups Veal Jus (see page 287) or Bouillon de Poule (see page 282)

1   Using a sharp knife, trim and remove any fat, gristle, and silver skin from the beef.

2   Cut the fatback lengthwise into ¼-inch-wide strips. Using a larding needle, gently thread the fat evenly throughout the meat. If you do not feel comfortable larding the meat, ask your butcher to do it.

3   Place the meat in a large, deep, nonreactive dish and cover with the chopped onion, carrot, leek and garlic. Toss in the thyme, parsley, and bay leaf. Pour 4 cups of the red wine over the top, taking care that the meat is completely submerged. Cover with plastic film and refrigerate for 1 week.

4   The night prior to cooking, remove the meat from the marinade, separately reserving the marinade. Wrap the meat and cover the marinade with plastic film, and return both to the refrigerator.

5   When ready to cook, preheat the oven to 350°F.

6   Heat the duck fat in an ovenproof braising pan with a cover over medium heat. Add the diced onions, and sweat for about 5 minutes or until they are soft, taking care that they do not brown or color. Add the tomato paste and flour and, stirring constantly, cook for 5 minutes.

7   Season the meat on both sides with salt and pepper to taste. Place the meat, along with the remaining red wine and the reserved marinade, in the pan. Raise the heat and bring to a simmer. Cook for about 20 minutes or until the liquid has reduced by half. Add the pork rind and Veal Jus. Cover and place in the preheated oven and cook for 1½ hours or until the meat is fork tender. Remove from the oven and carefully transfer the meat to a platter. Cover with a warm, moist kitchen towel to keep the meat from drying out.

8   Remove and discard the pork rind from the sauce.

9   Place the braising liquid over medium heat and bring to a simmer. Simmer for about 20 minutes or until the liquid has reduced by half, skimming off any scum or fat that may rise to the surface. Pass the sauce through a fine mesh sieve into a clean saucepan, discarding the solids. Keep warm.

10 Using a sharp knife, cut the meat, against the grain, into ¼-inch-thick slices. Place the meat on a serving platter and spoon the warm sauce over the top. Serve immediately.

Carbonnade de boeuf flamande

BEEF BRAISED WITH BEER AND ONIONS

SERVES 4

Carbonnade refers to both this dish and a style of cooking over an open coal or wood fire. This dish of beef cooked in beer and onions comes from Flanders. It often has a bit of brown sugar added to give a hint of sweetness to the aromatic beer or ale. Finished with a crust of golden breadcrumbs, it is a rich and filling meal. Again, this is a dish that highlights the art of braising and the craft of a saucier—an art and a craft that I continue to hone.

3½ to 4 pounds rump steak or bottom round, cut lengthwise into 3-ounce pieces

Coarse salt to taste

Freshly ground pepper to taste

½ cup all-purpose flour

½ pound duck fat

⅜ cup light olive oil

5 onions, peeled and sliced

5 cloves garlic, peeled and sliced

5 bottles amber ale

8 cups Veal Jus (see page 287)

1 Bouquet Garni (see page 293)

3 tablespoons tomato paste

½ cup fresh breadcrumbs (see page 299)

1 Preheat the oven to 350°F.

2 Tenderize and flatten the meat with a meat cleaver or meat hammer. Cut each flat-tened piece into ½-inch-thick slices. Season the meat with salt and pepper to taste.

3 Place the flour on a plate and press each piece of meat into the flour, lightly coating both sides. Gently pat the meat with a paper towel to remove any excess flour.

4 Heat the duck fat in a large sauté pan over high heat until it is almost smoking. Add the meat and sauté for about 3 minutes or until golden brown on all sides. Remove the meat from the pan and reserve. Drain and reserve the excess fat.

5 Heat the olive oil in a large braising pan with a cover over medium heat. Add the onions and garlic, and sweat for 5 minutes or until they are translucent, taking care that they do not brown or color.

6 Using a slotted spoon, remove the onions and the garlic from the pan and set aside. Add the ale and, using a wooden spoon, stir to deglaze the pan. Stir in the Veal Jus and Bouquet Garni. Raise the heat and bring to a boil. Immediately drain off and reserve all of the liquid.

7 Arrange half of the reserved onion and garlic in the bottom of the braising pan. Cover the onions with all of the meat; then make a layer of the remaining onions and garlic. Stir the tomato paste into the reserved ale-Veal Jus mixture and then pour the mixture over the meat. Cover and place in the preheated oven, and braise for 2 to 3 hours or until the meat is fork tender. Remove from the oven and let stand, covered, for 20 min-utes. Do not turn off the oven.

8 Using a slotted spoon, carefully transfer the meat and onions into an 11½-inch by 4-inch baking dish.

9 Place the braising liquid on the stove top over medium heat and bring to a simmer. Simmer for 15 minutes, skimming off any scum or impurities that rise to the surface. Immediately, pass the braising liquid through a fine mesh sieve and reserve. Taste and, if necessary, adjust the seasoning with salt and pepper. Pour just enough of the hot braising liquid over the meat and the onions to cover.

10 Sprinkle the breadcrumbs over the top. Place in the preheated oven and bake for about 25 minutes or until a golden crust forms on top. Serve immediately.

Tarte tatin

UPSIDE-DOWN APPLE TART

> SERVES 6

This is the famous classic upside-down apple tart, which is cooked in a sauté pan until it is well caramelized with the pastry crust on top. After the tart is cooked, you flip it over onto a plate to put the crust on the bottom. In the Café, I would watch the pastry cooks with fascination as they made the caramel directly in the pan with the apples.

3 pounds apples, peeled

1 cup sugar

½ cup unsalted butter

½ pound commercial puff pastry

½ cup crème fraîche, optional

1   Cut the apples in half and core them; then cut lengthwise into quarters.

2   Preheat the oven to 350°F.

3   Place the sugar in a heavy-duty nonstick saucepan over medium heat. Cook, stirring frequently with a wooden spoon and brushing down the sides of the pan with a clean pastry brush, for about 15 minutes or until the sugar is golden brown and nicely caramelized. Beat in the butter with a wooden spoon. Pour the hot caramel into a 10-inch round mold.

4   Place the apples in the mold, side by side, in concentric circles, fitting them in tightly. Place in the preheated oven and bake for 50 minutes or until the apples caramelize and almost melt. Remove from the oven and place on a wire rack; allow to come to room temperature.

5   Again, preheat the oven to 350°F.

6   Roll the puff pastry out on a lightly floured surface to a very thin circle. Cut the pastry into a 10-inch circle that will cover the apples. Place the pastry on top of the apples to make a neat fit. Place in the preheated oven and bake for 30 minutes or until the puff pastry is crisp and golden brown. Remove from the oven and place on a wire rack to cool for 3 hours.

7   When ready to serve, preheat the oven to 300°F.

8   Turn the mold out onto an ovenproof serving plate and place in the oven to reheat. When just warm, remove from the oven and cut into serving pieces. Serve warm with a dollop of crème fraîche on each serving, if desired.

maneuvers when my nose caught a familiar aroma that pulled me into the forest, where I came upon a farmer and his wife with their pig on a leash and a truffle the size of an apple in hand. The night under the stars after a jump into the mountains, drinking a farmer's homemade chilled white wine with a perfectly fresh, grassy taste that lingers with me still.

After being discharged from the army in 1967, I needed to get back into the kitchen. I decided to return to Montreal, where I got a job in a very prestigious country club working as the *sous chef* under Robert Joly. I spent this time learning the *garde-manger* (cold food station) and the art of *chaud-froid* (decorating cooked meats and poultry with aspic and vegetable garnish). Although I enjoyed the experience, I was anxious to learn more and after one season I moved on to a large restaurant with a huge, old-fashioned brigade. I worked as the *chef saucier* and sous chef, making sauces and braising meats and supervising the crew. It was a terrific learning experience. However, in 1969 an opportunity came my way that I couldn't pass by. I was offered a chef saucier position in Freeport, Grand Bahamas. A snowy winter in Montreal or the beaches of the Caribbean? I made a quick choice for the sun and sand! I gained invaluable experience in the kitchen during my one season in the sun but I also had a lot of fun. Soon it was time to move on for more learning, and I headed back to Montreal and the kitchen of St. Amable, one of the best restaurants in town.

After a few months in the restaurant, I happened to overhear a conversation between the owner, M.Garcin, and an American innkeeper who was looking for a chef for his restaurant. Since I had dreamed of going to America from the first moment I saw a John Wayne movie as a kid, I asked M.Garcin if I could look into the possibility of the job. With his blessing, my friend Robert Joly and I drove down to see the Swiss Hutte in Hillsdale, New York. Before I knew it, I had packed my meager possessions into my red Cortina GT and headed to the United States for my first job as *chef de cuisine*.

The Swiss Hutte was located just a few miles from the foothills of the Catamount Ski Area and was open seven days a week, ten months of the year, serving breakfast, lunch, and dinner every day except Monday. The owners, Tom and Linda Breen, became my patrons, with Tom overseeing the kitchen and Linda the front of the house. Because Linda loved making breakfast, I did not have to do the early morning cooking. But I was always in the kitchen at that time and I was awestruck by her ability to cook, flipping eggs and pancakes, wearing beautiful, expensive dresses with never a spot landing on her clothes! A feat that I could never accomplish!

I learned so many lessons at the Swiss Hutte as I adjusted to my new life with an American boss, a new language, and working with unskilled apprentices and unknown palates. From Tom, I learned that honesty and integrity were of the utmost importance when running a business. He always tried to please his customers but he also kept the ratio of quality to price uppermost in his mind. I learned to translate my menu to American tastes and still cook foods that were interesting to me as I became aware that American diners were not used to the more adventurous dishes that were familiar to the French table. Frogs' legs and rabbit weren't very successful but a wild boar civet dish was an unexpected hit. Every day I learned a new lesson!

I grew to love the countryside around the inn. Situated on the border between New York and Massachusetts, the farmland and rural setting reminded me of Gascony. Although the local products weren't always those that I knew from home, I still used everything that grew around the inn—I searched out any home-grown produce, meat and poultry, and dairy products that I could get my hands on. The fact that one of the neighboring restaurant owners was Jean Morel, a Frenchman who had worked in New York City for years before opening his own spot in Hillsdale, made it even more homelike for me. It was he who gave me insight into the restaurant business in the Big Apple, which, I somehow knew, was going to be my next stop.

I stayed at the Swiss Hutte for three and a half years, longer than I had ever worked in one place. I have to admit that it wasn't because I loved the job or the countryside so much; it was because of Mary Dunn, who was to become my wife. Mary was raised on a farm in Hillsdale and was working her way through college with a waitress job at the restaurant when we met. Her family reminded me so much of mine; the Dunns grew many of their own vegetables and raised their own livestock, and John, Mary's dad, made delicious apple cider from apples that were picked from trees on the farm. I embraced their wonderful life then, and all these years later I still enjoy our times together, making cider in the fall and bottling it in the spring.

While Mary finished her studies, I decided that I should move on with my career. Since I didn't want to venture far from Mary, New York City seemed the best choice for advancement. A friend of mine arranged for an interview with Michel Ratte, the chef of Le Chateau Richelieu on 52nd Street between Madison and

Park. I was hired to be the evening sous chef-saucier, and I started immediately. I loved the excitement of the city and the network of chefs available to me. I had always wanted to work in New York but had been a bit afraid because it seemed so grandiose. It was strange to find it so welcoming, and these years became some of the best of my life.

Mary and I married in 1974 and, since she was teaching, I decided to try to find a chef's job that would give me more regular hours so that I could spend more time with my new bride. Besides, I thought I could use a little break after so many years of working long, long shifts as I learned my trade. I was lucky enough to find a job with Air France, working under Michel Martin, their executive chef. Unbelievable as it might seem, it was during this time that I gained most of my knowledge about creating *haute cuisine;* at this point, the food served in First Class rivaled the finest restaurants in the world, due to the vision of Chef Martin. He had the advantage of experiencing the *Tour de France,* which, to French cooks, is not the famous bicycle race but a series of kitchen jobs over several years revolving through each province of France. After the young cook had worked for a period of time in one restaurant, the cooperating chef would send him on to the next restaurant. The knowledge that he had gained on the Tour and by working at such prestigious Parisian restaurants as Lucas Carton was put in place to serve the passengers of the airline and to teach his staff. I learned many techniques related to cold preparation: pâtés, terrines, galantines, and foie gras presentations. Michel was a master at making *pâté en croûte* and *jambon en croûte,* using the dough as a tool for decoration. He truly understood the science of gastronomy and used it to make a restaurant in the sky!

I stayed with Air France for a few years and then went on to the world-famous Windows on the World, which, sadly, was destroyed in the 2001 terrorist attack on the World Trade Center. At that time, the restaurant was a huge operation with almost 100 cooks in the kitchen, and I was third man in charge. The menu was more American than French, with James Beard, who worked with us, involved in planning the menu. From Windows, I returned to Air France to work on the restaurant for the new Concorde and then on to work in Paris with the highly acclaimed chef of "nouvelle cuisine," Alain Senderens, at his three-star restaurant L'Archestrate. After I had been there for a short time, Chef Senderens, working as a chef-consultant, sent me to be the opening chef de cuisine at the Maurice Restaurant in the Parker Meridien Hotel on 56th Street in Manhattan.

I was extremely excited to take on this new challenge. I worked hard and had some wonderful young chefs, such as the now well-known Ed Brown and Michael Colameco, working for me. I am proud to say that we were awarded three stars from *The New York Times* in 1986, setting a new standard for hotel dining. "For the first time, a hotel restaurant makes it to the Forbes top—Maurice" declared the four-star rating in *Forbes Magazine* in 1985. My old friend Jean Louis Palladin paid me a visit one night and, sampling the food, said, "Your food is still underseasoned," while I countered, "And yours is still overseasoned"—our comfortable, joking friendship sealed in hotel school was still in place even as we had moved along in our chosen careers.

During my tenure at L'Archestrate I had become very involved in the evolution of nouvelle cuisine, for which Chef Senderens had gained much notoriety. He was so successful at this innovation because he built his new direction on a firm base of classical French cooking. It was as though he had the engine and the wheels and then put a new chassis on top of them to create a more refined vision of the classics that would drive us into the culinary future. He seemed to know instinctively how to take a recipe to its next and often lighter stage. He worked within the confines of terroir but his adventuresome palate allowed him to introduce foreign and unfamiliar ingredients into the classic French repertoire. For instance, with *Canard Epicius* he knew how to use the fat content of the duck as it roasted with honey and exotic spices to make the final dish better without being fatty or greasy. Creating his classic lobster and vanilla combination, he found that the less the lobster cooked, the sweeter the meat, and the vanilla-scented *beurre blanc* simply served to highlight the sweetness more intensely.

At the Maurice, I took all that Chef Senderens had taught me and built further on my classical culinary education. He really taught me how to navigate the classic repertoire through different waters, allowing that a chef should never introduce any ingredient that did not make sense to the entire recipe. He taught me to look at the number of ingredients, their texture and taste, and the importance of artistry on the plate. I would say that he had a very strong influence on my development as a chef. During my years at the Maurice, I tried to heed Chef Senderens' advice to follow the recipes that I knew from L'Archestrate but to make them my own. It is a philosophy that stayed with me long after my association with the chef ended.

Raviolis de St. Jacques, Thym et Courgettes
SCALLOP RAVIOLIS WITH ZUCCHINI AND THYME

Ravioli de Céleri Boule et Truffes
CELERY AND TRUFFLE RAVIOLI

Salade de Homard, Mesclun, Gratons de Canard et Mangue
LOBSTER SALAD WITH DUCK AND MANGO

Légumes en Barigoule Provençaux
VEGETABLES COOKED IN WHITE WINE AND HERBS

Purée de Patates Douces
CARAMELIZED SWEET POTATOES WITH BANANA

Asperges et Morilles
ASPARAGUS AND MUSHROOMS

Fenouil à la Crème de Curry
FENNEL WITH CURRIED CREAM

Petit Pois à la Française
FRESH PEAS, FRENCH STYLE

Alicuit de Canard, Carottes, et Pommes de Terre
CARROT AND POTATO COOKED WITH DUCK

Pigeon Rôti Fèves, Oignons, Grelots, Asperges, Coulis de Pois
ROASTED SQUAB WITH VEGETABLES AND PEA SAUCE

Civet de Lièvre
BRAISED HARE WITH RED WINE

Venaison Poilée, dans son Jus Parfumé à la Framboise, Choux au Poivre Rose
PAN-ROASTED VENISON WITH RASPBERRY SAUCE AND CABBAGE WITH PINK PEPPERCORNS

Selle d'Agneau Rôtie à l'Os, Crème l'Estragon
LAMB ROASTED ON THE BONE WITH CREAM OF TARRAGON

Raviolis de St. Jacques,

SCALLOP RAVIOLIS WITH ZUCCHINI AND THYME

thym et courgettes

> ● SERVES 4

Alain Senderens traveled frequently to the Far East and his trips brought new ideas and inspired ingredients to French cooking. Because of the chef's adventurous palate and creativity, in 1982 we were the first to use wonton skin wrappers to make raviolis in New York City. Now, it's an almost everyday occurrence in the city's restaurants.

The original recipe was made with petoncles, which, for want of a more scientific definition, are basically a very small type of scallop. Only available from September to November on the east coast, they are usually very difficult to find in the United States. You may be able to find them in the fall at a very good fishmonger; however, the more readily available small bay scallops are an excellent substitute.

3 ounces whole petoncles or finely diced bay scallops

2½ teaspoons fresh thyme leaves

Coarse salt to taste

Freshly ground pepper to taste

4 zucchini, well washed and trimmed

1 large egg

½ teaspoon water

24 wonton skins

5 tablespoons Beurre Blanc (see page 290)

4 sprigs thyme

1   Combine the petoncles (or scallops) and 2 teaspoons of the thyme with salt and pepper to taste. Let rest for 10 minutes.

2   Peel the zucchini into strips about 5 inches long, ¾ inches thick, and ¾ inches wide. Cut each strip, on the bias, into ½-inch-wide pieces. You will need 12 perfect zucchini pieces.

3   Bring a small saucepan of salted water to boil over high heat. Add the zucchini pieces and blanch for about 45 seconds. Drain well and place under cold, running water to stop the cooking. Pat dry and set aside.

4   Whisk the egg and water together. When well blended, set aside.

5   Line a baking sheet with parchment paper and set aside.

6   Lay 12 wonton skins out on a clean dry surface. Place 1½ teaspoons of the scallops in the center of each wonton skin. Place a piece of the zucchini on top of the scallops and using a pastry brush, lightly coat the edges of the wonton skins with the egg wash. Cover each filled wonton skin with one of the remaining wonton skins. Press down firmly with your fingers on all sides to form a tight seal around the scallop mixture. Using a 2½-inch round cookie cutter that fits easily over the scallop mound cut the raviolis into circles, leaving an edge of about a quarter inch. Place the raviolis on the prepared baking sheet, cover with parchment paper and place in the refrigerator for 1 hour or until well chilled.

7   Place the Beurre Blanc in the top half of a double boiler over boiling water. Place over medium heat and add the remaining ½ teaspoon thyme. Heat, stirring frequently, for 3 minutes or until the sauce is warm. Remove from the heat and keep warm.

8   Bring a large pot of salted water to a rolling boil.

9   Remove the raviolis from the refrigerator. Uncover and drop the raviolis into the boiling water. Boil for 2 minutes or until they are soft and translucent. Using a slotted spoon, remove the raviolis from the water and place on a double layer of paper towels to drain well.

10 Place the raviolis in a shallow dish. Add the warm Beurre Blanc and stir gently to very lightly coat. Using a slotted spoon, transfer 3 raviolis to each of four plates. Garnish with a sprig of thyme and serve immediately.

Ravioli de céleri boule

CELERY AND TRUFFLE RAVIOLI

et truffes

● SERVES 4

This dish is a perfect example of Alain Senderens' creativity in pairing out-of-the-ordinary combinations. In this instance, celery root, an inexpensive and common root vegetable, is matched with the rare and expensive truffle. Although most cooks would probably never think of putting these disparate foods together, Senderens instinctively knew that they were made for each other. He knew that the subtle anise scent of the celery root would accentuate the earthy and slightly sensual flavor of the truffle. It was quite a revelation for me to discover how complementary the two were to each another. It was such a superb mix that I have continued to create a variation of this flavor combination over the years with a puree of celery root accented with diced truffles and truffle oil my most recent innovation.

2 tablespoons unsalted butter

1 cup celery root chopped into ¼-inch dice

¼ cup black truffles chopped into ¼-inch dice

¼ teaspoon coarse salt plus more to taste

Freshly ground pepper to taste

1 large egg

1½ teaspoons water

24 wonton skins

2 tablespoons truffle juice

1 cup Beurre Blanc (see page 290)

1 large black truffle

2 teaspoons light olive oil or black truffle oil

Approximately ¼ teaspoon fleur de sel

1. Heat the butter in a medium sauté pan over medium-high heat. Add the celery root and sweat for 3 to 5 minutes or until just soft, taking care that it does not brown. Add the diced truffles and continue to sauté for 2 to 3 minutes. Season with salt and pepper to taste. Remove from the heat and allow to cool to room temperature.

2. Whisk the egg and water together in a small bowl. When well blended, set aside.

3. Lay out 12 wonton skins on a clean, dry surface. Place 1½ teaspoons of the cooled celery-truffle mixture in the center of each wonton skin.

4. Using a pastry brush, lightly coat the edges of the wonton skins with the egg wash. Cover each filled wonton skin with one of the remaining wonton skins, pressing firmly on all sides with your fingertips to form a tight seal. Using a 2-inch round cookie cutter cut the raviolis into circles having about a ¼-inch edge.

5. Place the raviolis on a baking sheet. Cover with parchment paper and place in the refrigerator for 1 hour or until well chilled.

6. Place the truffle juice in a small saucepan over high heat and bring to a simmer. Lower the heat and simmer for 3 minutes or until reduced by half.

7. Place the Beurre Blanc on the side of the stove top. Whisk in the reduced truffle juice and reduce the heat to very low to just keep the sauce warm.

8. Using a mandoline or a Japanese vegetable slicer (a Benriner) cut the whole truffle into twelve ⅛-inch-thick slices. Place the truffle slices in a small mixing bowl and add the oil. Toss lightly to coat.

9. Bring a large pot of salted water to a rolling boil.

10. Remove the raviolis from the refrigerator. Uncover and drop the raviolis into the boiling water. Boil for 2 minutes or until they are soft and translucent. Using a slotted spoon, remove the raviolis from the water and place on a double layer of paper towels to drain.

12. Transfer the raviolis to a shallow dish. Add the warm truffle sauce and stir gently to coat. Using a slotted spoon, transfer 3 raviolis to each of four plates. Place a truffle slice on top of each ravioli and finish with a few grains of fleur de sel. Serve immediately.

Salade de homard, mesclun,

LOBSTER SALAD WITH DUCK

gratons de canard,

AND MANGO

et mangue

● SERVES 4

Here again, unexpected ingredients are combined for a surprising but sublime taste. Gratons are small squares of meat with a thick layer of skin or fat on them that have been cooked slowly in a sauté pan. The fat accumulates in the pan and then crisps the meat and makes it very succulent. This method of preparation is similar in concept to a confit. Gratons are usually made from either a leg of pork or duck. In Gascony, they are very commonly served as an hors d'oeuvre with aperitifs. And quite often they are tossed into salads as meaty croutons.

Alain Senderens' original recipe had only the gratons of duck. In my version of the dish I use both gratons and slices of roasted duck breast so that the two textures will add another layer of interest to the dish. The duck breast remains very soft and juicy while the gratons are crispy and crunchy, which make a very pleasant contrast with the salad. For the greens, I like to use a mix of burgundy raddichio, yellow leaves of Italian frisée, and the soft green of slightly sweet mâche.

Two 1¼-pound lobsters

1 tablespoon coarse salt plus more to taste

One 3-pound female Muscovy duck

½ tablespoon unsalted butter, at room temperature

1 tablespoon light olive oil

10 tablespoons olive oil

2 tablespoons Banyuls vinegar

1 tablespoon champagne vinegar

1 tablespoon water

Freshly ground pepper to taste

6 ounces frisée, yellow part only, trimmed, well washed and dried

3 ounces mâche, trimmed and washed

3 ounces radicchio, torn into bite-size pieces, well washed and dried

¼ cup chopped shallots

1 tablespoon julienned fresh flat-leaf parsley

1 teaspoon chopped fresh chives

1 teaspoon coarsely chopped chervil

Zest of 1 orange, blanched

2 half-ripe mangos, peeled, seeded, and cut into fine julienne

Eight 3-inch-long by ½-inch-wide carrot strips

10 basil leaves, julienned

1   Bring a stockpot of salted water to boil over high heat. Add the lobsters and again bring to a boil. Boil for 7 to 8 minutes or until the lobsters are bright red. Remove the lobsters from the water and set aside to cool to room temperature.

2   When the lobsters are cool enough to handle, separate the tail and claws from the body. Crack the shell, and carefully remove the meat from the claws and tails, taking care that the meat remains in whole pieces. Slice the tails crosswise into 1-inch-thick medallions and cut the claw meat into ¼-inch dice. Place the tail and claw meat on separate plates, cover, and refrigerate.

3   Preheat the oven to 375°F.

4   Using 1 tablespoon of salt, generously season the cavity of the duck and truss it according to the directions on page 261.

5   Spread the butter and then ½ tablespoon of the light olive oil evenly over the skin of the duck. Place the duck on a rack in a roasting pan in the preheated oven and roast for 30 minutes or until an instant-read thermometer inserted at the thigh joint reads 110°F. Remove the duck from the oven and let rest at room temperature for 20 minutes. Reduce the oven temperature to 200°F.

6   Using a sharp knife, remove the legs from the duck by pulling the legs out toward you and cutting down along the bone. Cut the leg meat into ¼-inch dice and set it aside. Carefully remove each breast half and set aside.

7   Heat the remaining ½ tablespoon of light olive oil in a large sauté pan over medium heat. When the oil is hot but not smoking, add the diced duck meat and fry for 10 minutes or until crispy and golden brown. Using a slotted spoon, lift the duck meat to a double layer of paper towels to drain well.

8   Whisk together the olive oil, Banyuls vinegar, champagne vinegar, and water until well blended. Season with salt and pepper to taste and set aside.

9   Combine the lobster meat with 3 tablespoons of the vinaigrette in a small ovenproof dish. Place in the preheated oven for 2 to 3 minutes or until just warmed through. Do not turn off the oven.

10 Combine the frisée, mâche, radicchio, shallots, parsley, chives, and chervil. Toss with 3 tablespoons of the reserved vinaigrette. Add the diced duck and lobster meat along with the orange zest. Season with salt and pepper to taste.

11 Place the duck breast on an ovenproof dish in the preheated oven for 3 minutes or until just warmed through. Cut lengthwise into ¼-inch-thick slices.

12 Place an equal portion of the mixed salad on each of four plates. Arrange an equal portion of lobster tail medallions around the greens on each plate. Place 4 slices of duck breast on top of each salad along with 4 pieces of julienne mango, 2 carrot strips and a sprinkle of basil julienne. Serve immediately.

Légumes en barigoule

VEGETABLES COOKED IN WHITE WINE AND HERBS

Provençaux

● SERVES 4

In the summer, Provence is like one huge vegetable garden. The bounty of that garden is highlighted in this almost traditional recipe: baby artichokes, tender carrots and turnips, luscious unfiltered olive oil, and piquant lemon juice. This dish is attractive not only because of its fresh and colorful presentation but also for its forthright flavor. It is a wonderful by itself but it also works well as a side dish for veal, grilled fish, and poultry. The sunny warmth of Provence will flourish in your kitchen when you recreate this healthful dish.

½ cup plus 3 tablespoons extra-virgin olive oil

4 fingerling potatoes, washed, peeled, cut into a ½-inch dice, and blanched

Coarse salt to taste

Freshly ground pepper to taste

1 onion, peeled and chopped

10 ounces bacon, blanched and cut to a 2-inch dice

10 baby artichokes, cleaned

10 baby fennel bulbs, cleaned

8 baby carrots, cleaned and peeled

6 cloves garlic, peeled and crushed

4 spring onions, cleaned, keeping some of the stems

2 tablespoons fresh thyme leaves

1 pinch ground star anise

2 cups light Bouillon de Poule (see page 282)

½ cup white wine

3 tablespoons fresh lemon juice

4 tomatoes, peeled, cored, seeded and quartered

3 ounces haricots verts, trimmed of two ends and blanched

2 ounces fava beans, blanched

2 ounces English peas, barely blanched

1 tablespoon flat-leaf parsley, julienne

1   Preheat the oven to 375°F.

2   Heat 2 tablespoons of the olive oil in an ovenproof sauté pan over medium heat. Add the potatoes and sauté for 5 minutes or until they are just browning. Season with salt and pepper to taste. Place the potatoes in the preheated oven and bake for about 15 minutes or until they are crisp on the outside and tender and creamy on the inside. Remove from the oven and set aside.

3   Heat ½ cup of the remaining olive oil in a shallow creuset-style braising pan with a cover over medium heat. Add the chopped onion and sweat for about 5 minutes, taking care that it does not brown. Reduce the heat to medium-low and add the bacon, artichokes, fennel, carrots, garlic, and spring onions. Season with salt and pepper to taste and continue to cook, stirring frequently, for 10 minutes. Add the thyme and star anise. Cover and reduce the heat to low. Cook for 5 minutes. Uncover and add the Bouillon de Poule, white wine, and lemon juice. Cook, uncovered, for about 7 minutes or until the vegetables are tender. Add the tomatoes, raise the heat and bring to a boil. Immediately, lower the heat and simmer for 3 minutes.

4   Strain the vegetables through fine sieve, reserving the liquid. Place the vegetables in a bowl and keep warm.

5   Return the liquid to the braising pan and bring to a boil over high heat. Boil for about 15 minutes or until the liquid is reduced by half. Season with salt and pepper to taste. Return the vegetables to the pan and stir gently.

6   Drain the oil from the potatoes and add them to the other vegetables.

7   Heat the remaining tablespoon of olive oil in the same pan used to cook the potatoes. Add the haricots verts, fava beans, and peas and sauté for 3 minutes. Stir into the vegetable mixture. Spoon equal portions of the vegetables into each of four shallow soup bowls. Garnish the top with parsley and serve.

Purée de patates douces

CARAMELIZED SWEET POTATOES WITH BANANA

● SERVES 4

We often used this recipe as an accompaniment for game dishes at the Maurice. This is yet another example of Senderens' genius in combining flavors. Sweet potatoes themselves are fairly bland with a very simple sweet, starchy taste, but the addition of bananas and apples gives a whole new dimension to the flavor. The sweetness of the caramel reinforces the sweetness of the fruits and the potato while the acidity of the orange juice creates just the right balance for the union. This is my preferred Thanksgiving sweet potato dish, especially with a spit-roasted wild turkey. However, it is also a great complement to any roasted white meat or poultry.

⅓ cup granulated sugar

½ cup water

Juice of ½ orange

1 pound sweet potatoes, peeled and cut into 1-inch cubes

1 teaspoon unsalted butter

1 apple, peeled, cored, and cut into pieces

1 banana, peeled and cut crosswise into ½-inch-thick pieces

1 tablespoon crème fraîche

juice of ½ lemon

1 teaspoon confectioners' sugar

I   Combine the granulated sugar and water in a medium skillet over medium heat. Bring to a boil; then reduce the heat and simmer for 15 minutes or until a light brown caramel color. Carefully, add the orange juice to stop the caramel from cooking. Stir in the sweet potatoes and continue to cook for 25 minutes or until fork tender.

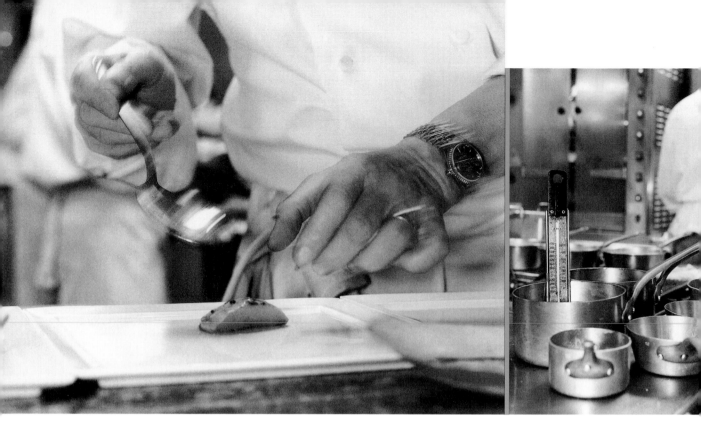

2   Drain the sweet potatoes through a colander, reserving the liquid. Transfer the liquid to a small saucepan over medium heat and bring to a simmer. Simmer, stirring occasionally, for 10 minutes or until reduced by half.

3   Transfer the sweet potatoes to the bowl of a food processor fitted with the metal blade and process for 1 minute or until smooth. Add the reduced cooking liquid to the puree and process to blend. Scrape the mixture from the processor and set aside.

4   Combine the butter and apple in a medium sauté pan over medium-high heat. Sauté for 8 minutes or until fork tender. Stir in the banana and cook for an additional 3 minutes or until the banana is very soft. Remove from the heat and let rest for 5 minutes.

5   Transfer the apple-banana mixture to a food processor fitted with the metal blade and process for 1 minute or until smooth. Add the reserved sweet potatoes and process to just blend. Add the crème fraîche and briefly process to combine. (Sweet potatoes can be fibrous, so if the mixture seems stringy, push it through a fine sieve to smooth out.)

6   Transfer the mixture to a serving bowl. Stir in the lemon juice and confectioners' sugar and serve.

Oignon farci PAGE 215

Le risotto de homard et truffes noires

PAGE 220

Ragoût de légumes miniatures mijotés à l'huile d'olive, truffes, et sel gris   PAGE 237

Saumon confit à l'huile d'olive, salade de roquettes, vinaigre de balsamique

PAGE 246

Langoustines poêlées aus truffes, mousseline de choux-fleur

PAGE 252

Homard poché en coque, avec son bouillon réduit à l'éstragon, carottes à l'écrasées PAGE 248

Asperges et morilles

ASPARAGUS AND MUSHROOMS

● SERVES 4

Morels pop out of the earth at the first sign of spring, bursting with intense flavor. Asparagus is not far behind, pushing its tender green stalks up through the loam. So morels and asparagus combined are the perfect welcome to spring—fresh, healthy, and très èlegante. The textures are so different— asparagus firm and slightly crisp and morels spongy and chewy.

In America, we have blonde morels that grow in the Pacific Northwest. They are somewhat less tasty than the more expensive almost-black morels I knew in France. Whatever type you use, they should be firm, with stems intact and no bruising. Morels are quite sandy and need to be well cleaned. Just before using, remove the stems and wash them three times in cold water to which you have added a few drops of vinegar to kill any insects.

This is a perfect garnish for a grilled veal chop, sweetbreads, grilled rabbit, or roast chicken. It could also be served as an appetizing prelude to a simple dinner. Cut the asparagus into smaller pieces, and you will have an absolutely delicious garnish for a soft, runny omelet to serve at a most luxurious brunch.

8 to 10 jumbo stalks green asparagus

¼ cup light olive oil

3 tablespoons unsalted butter

5 shallots, peeled and finely diced

3 tablespoons chopped fresh flat-leaf parsley

Coarse salt to taste

Freshly ground pepper to taste

16 morels, cleaned

¼ cup crème fraîche

1   Cut off the hard white bottom from each asparagus stalk, leaving a stalk about 5 to 6 inches long. Using a vegetable peeler, peel off the tough outer skin, taking care not to remove too much of the flesh.

2   Bring a large pot of salted water to a boil over high heat. Add the asparagus and cook for about 4 minutes or until al dente. Drain well and refresh under cold running water. Pat dry.

3   Heat the olive oil in a sauté pan over medium high heat. Add the asparagus and sauté for about 4 minutes or until they are a golden brown color on all sides. Remove the pan from the heat and drain off all of the oil. Add 1 tablespoon of the butter and half of the shallots and parsley, and stir to combine. Season with salt and pepper to taste. Transfer to a serving platter and tent lightly with aluminum foil to keep warm.

4   Place the same sauté pan over medium heat. Add the remaining 2 tablespoons of butter and heat for 3 minutes or until it begins to foam. Add the morels and season with salt and pepper to taste. Sauté for 5 minutes or until just soft. Stir in the remaining shallots and parsley along with the crème fraîche. Remove from the heat.

5   Remove the foil from the asparagus. Fan out the asparagus *au flute* on the platter and spoon the morels over the top. Serve warm.

Fenouil à la crème de curry

FENNEL WITH CURRIED CREAM

● SERVES 4

The fresh, spicy-sweet licorice taste of the fennel is a terrific partner to the curry. In fact, many curry mixes have a percentage of toasted fennel seed, so the theme is already set. The fennel gives a hint of sweet spice and the turmeric in the curry powder infuses a wonderful yellow color into the vegetables cooked in it.

I think that this combination is particularly well suited to bringing out the rich, fatty flavor of spring lamb. However, beyond its lamb match, this combination gives a marvelous accent to veal, poultry, or grilled fish. It also makes a beautiful vegetarian brunch dish.

3 tablespoons light olive oil

¼ cup finely diced onion

3 tablespoons regular curry powder

¼ cup water

4 medium fennel bulbs, washed, stems trimmed, quartered, and blanched

2 cups heavy cream

Coarse salt to taste

Freshly ground pepper to taste

1 Preheat the oven to 450°F.

2 Heat 2 tablespoons of the olive oil in a large sauté pan over medium heat. Add the onions and sweat for 2 minutes or until they are translucent, taking care that they do not brown. Add the curry powder and continue cooking as you stir in the water. Bring to a simmer and simmer for 5 minutes. Remove from the heat and scrape into a mixing bowl. Set aside.

3 Using a pastry brush and the remaining 1 tablespoon of olive oil, lightly coat the bottom of an oval baking dish large enough to hold the fennel in a single layer. Fit the fennel into the dish and set aside.

4 Place the heavy cream in a medium saucepan over medium heat and cook just until bubbles form around the edge of the pan. Lower the heat and cook at a bare simmer for 5 minutes. Stir in the reserved curried onions. Season with salt and pepper to taste and simmer for an additional 5 minutes. Remove from the heat and pass through a fine mesh sieve, discarding the solids.

5 Pour the seasoned cream over the fennel to cover by three-quarters. Place in the preheated oven and bake for about 7 minutes or until the fennel is cooked through and the sauce is bubbling. Raise the oven temperature to broil and immediately transfer the dish to the broiler. Broil for 3 minutes or until the top is golden brown. Serve immediately.

Petit pois à la Française

FRESH PEAS FRENCH STYLE

SERVES 4

Peas are, to me, almost like flowers, given their color, sweet aroma, and flowery flavor. They are so much the essence of the spring and summer with the shoots, tendrils, pods, and peas all adding their particular scent to the table. Along with asparagus and morels, peas signal spring on my menu. I often match their butter-sweet taste with gamy poultry such as squab. I also like to use them in cold soups that are bright green and fresh tasting. They sing with celebration of spring and summer.

Fresh peas should be eaten almost as soon as they are picked and should not be kept in their shells for more than 12 hours. If you have to keep them longer, shell, mix with 3 ounces of softened butter, cover, and refrigerate until ready to cook.

6 tablespoons unsalted butter

4 cups fresh English peas

1 head Boston lettuce, washed and quartered

2 teaspoons sugar

2 sprigs fresh chervil

1 sprig fresh flat-leaf parsley

12 pearl onions, peeled

3 tablespoons water

2 tablespoons chopped fresh chervil

Coarse salt

1   Cut ¼ cup of the butter into 1-inch cubes. Combine the cubed butter with the peas, Boston lettuce, and 1 teaspoon of the sugar, along with the chervil and parsley sprigs, in a mixing bowl. Cover with plastic film and refrigerate.

2   Combine the pearl onions and water with the remaining 2 tablespoons butter and 1 teaspoon sugar in a medium sauté pan over medium heat. Bring to a boil; then reduce the heat and simmer for about 7 minutes or until the onions are fork tender. Add the pea-lettuce mixture and cook, stirring constantly, for about 4 minutes or until the mixture comes to a boil. Immediately remove the pan from the heat.

3   Carefully remove and discard the parsley and chervil sprigs.

4   Remove and slice the Boston lettuce.

5   Place the peas and onions on a small serving platter and scatter the sliced lettuce over the top. Sprinkle the top with the chopped chervil and coarse salt to taste. Serve immediately.

Alicuit de canard, carottes, et

CARROT AND POTATO COOKED WITH DUCK

pommes de terre

SERVES 4

This is a real farm-style dish. In fact, in Gascony this would be a typical farmer's dish, with only the neck and wings of the duck used to add some meaty flavor and gelatin to the stew.

To move the everyday meal into haute cuisine, I use two parts of the duck to elevate the dish. The magret is cooked medium-rare and the wings are cooked as in the traditional stew. The carrots and potatoes should be cooked to a creamy texture but should still hold their shape. With some added turnips, the alicuit could be used as a side dish for a roasted duck.

Coarse salt to taste

Freshly ground pepper to taste

8 Moulard duck wings

1 tablespoon rendered duck fat

2 medium onions, peeled and cut into ¼-inch dice

1 tablespoon tomato paste

½ cup white wine

2 cups Bouillon de Poule (see page 282)

8 cloves garlic, peeled

2 carrots, peeled and cut into 2-inch cubes

2 Idaho potatoes, peeled and cut into 2-inch cubes

One 16-ounce duck breast

1   Preheat the oven to 350°F.

2   Salt and pepper the duck wings on all sides.

3   Heat the duck fat in an ovenproof 5-quart creuset-style pan with a cover over medium heat. Add the duck wings and sear for about 10 minutes or until golden brown on all sides. Remove the wings from the pan and set aside. Drain and reserve the fat from the pan.

4   Return the pan to medium heat and add the onions. Sweat the onions for 4 minutes or until they are soft, taking care that they do not brown. Stir in the tomato paste until well blended. Add the reserved duck wings and cook, stirring occasionally, for 5 minutes. Add the wine and, using a wooden spoon, stir to deglaze the pan. Bring to a simmer and simmer for 5 minutes or until the liquid is reduced by half. Add the Bouillon de Poule and garlic cloves. Cover and place in the preheated oven. Braise for 1½ to 2 hours or until the wings are fork tender.

5   Uncover and add the carrots and potatoes. Continue to braise for 25 to 30 minutes or until the potatoes and carrots are tender.

6   Remove the pan from the oven and carefully remove the duck wings and vegetables, separately placing them in 2 serving dishes. Cover each with a warm, damp dishtowel to keep warm.

7   Strain the liquid through a fine mesh sieve into a small, clean saucepan. Skim off and discard any fat or impurities that rise to the surface. Place over low heat to keep warm.

8   Preheat and oil the grill.

9   Season both sides of the duck breast with salt and pepper to taste and place the breast on the grill, skin side down. Grill for 8 minutes. Turn and grill for an additional 4 minutes on the other side for medium-rare. Remove from the grill and let rest for 4 minutes.

10   Place vegetables in center of each of four shallow plates. Place wings in front of vegetables.

11   Using a sharp knife, cut the duck breast crosswise into ½-inch strips and place an equal portion on top of vegetables in each bowl. Pour the sauce around the vegetables and serve immediately.

Pigeon rôti fèves, oignons,

ROASTED SQUAB WITH VEGETABLES

grelots, asperges, coulis de pois

AND PEA SAUCE

● SERVES 4

Pigeon with sweet peas is a textbook example of traditional French cooking. As in many classic recipes, rich, gamy meat is paired with something sweet as a defined contrast. In addition, peas have a tendency to absorb the flavorful meat juices, and this works particularly well with the succulent pigeon. The creamy butter adds just the right amount of balance to make the final flavor a union in paradise. This is an exemplary spring dish full of color and taste.

4 squab

Coarse salt to taste

Freshly ground pepper to taste

4 cloves garlic, peeled

4 sprigs fresh thyme

3 tablespoons light olive oil

11 tablespoons unsalted butter, room temperature

12 medium stalks green asparagus, blanched

3 ounces fava beans, shelled and blanched

12 pearl onions, peeled and blanched

2 teaspoons sugar

4 ounces frozen petit peas, thawed and blanched

4 ounces fresh English peas, blanched

½ cup warm Pigeon Jus (see page 287)

1 Preheat the oven to 475°F.

2 Rinse the squab under cold, running water and pat dry. Season the cavity with salt and pepper to taste. Place a garlic clove and a thyme sprig into each squab cavity and truss the squabs according to the directions on page 262. If not roasting immediately, place on a platter and refrigerate until ready to cook. (This can be done up to 2 hours before roasting.)

3 Heat the olive oil in a large sauté pan over medium heat. When the oil is hot but not smoking, add the squab and sear, turning frequently, for about 5 minutes or until golden brown on all sides. Transfer the squab to a large roasting pan. Put 1 tablespoon of butter on top of each bird. Place in the preheated oven and roast for 8 minutes. Reduce the heat to 425°F and continue to roast for another 7 minutes or until an instant-read thermometer inserted into the thickest part reads 140°F. Remove from the oven and let rest for 15 minutes.

4 Trim and peel the asparagus, leaving peeled 4-inch-long stalks. Set aside.

5 Peel and remove the white stems from the fava beans. Set aside.

6 Combine the pearl onions with a pinch of salt, the sugar, and 1 tablespoon of the remaining butter in a small shallow pan over medium heat. Add enough water to cover the onions by one-half and bring to a simmer. Lower the heat and slowly reduce the liquid, and cook for about 15 minutes or until the onions are nicely glazed. Remove from the heat and cover with a piece of parchment paper.

7 Place the thawed peas in a food processor fitted with the metal blade. Add the remaining butter and process to a smooth paste. Season with salt and pepper to taste. Set aside.

8 Bring a medium sauté pan of salted water to a boil over high heat. Add the asparagus, fava beans, and English peas and boil for about 2 minutes or until al dente. Remove from the heat and drain well. Return the vegetables to medium heat and add the reserved pea butter. Bring to a simmer, stirring occasionally. Season with salt and pepper to taste. Place the seasoned vegetables on a large serving platter.

9 Carve the squab into serving pieces and place on top of the vegetables. Drizzle any remaining squab jus around the edge of the platter, and serve immediately.

Civet de lièvre

BRAISED HARE WITH RED WINE

● SERVES 4

Wild brown hare from Scotland is available at specialty butchers throughout the United States from October to January. It must be packed fully dressed, not actually in the fur, as in France, where you have to clean and dress the hare yourself. It usually comes fresh and vacuum-sealed in a plastic bag with enough blood and juices remaining in the bag to finish the sauce for this dish. When ordering wild hare be sure to request that it remain vacuum-sealed in the bag, as this not only seals in the flavor but helps with the aging process desired for wild meat. When opening the bag, drain off and reserve the blood with 3 tablespoons of Armagnac. The brandy will keep the blood from clotting. Refrigerate or freeze the liver as it, too, will be required to finish the dish.

1 Scottish wild brown hare, blood and liver reserved

13 cloves garlic, peeled

2 onions, peeled and chopped

1 carrot, peeled, trimmed, and cut into 1-inch cubes

1 bay leaf

1 sprig fresh flat-leaf parsley

1 sprig fresh thyme

1 bottle red wine, rich in tannins

1 cup cognac

1 teaspoon freshly ground pepper plus more to taste

¼ cup olive oil

Coarse salt to taste

2½ tablespoons duck fat

3 onions, peeled and cut into ¼-inch dice

1 teaspoon tomato paste

3 tablespoons all-purpose flour

1 bottle red wine

1 carrot, peeled, trimmed, and cut lengthwise into thick slices

2½ cups of Veal Jus (see page 287)

2 ounces pork rind, blanched

2 ounces bacon, blanched and cubed

1 tablespoon light olive oil

9 pearl onions, peeled and blanched

1 rabbit liver, chopped

2 tablespoons unsalted butter

3 tablespoons Armagnac

1 teaspoon ground cloves

1 tablespoon chopped flat-leaf parsley

1   Cut the hare into 7 pieces: 2 hind legs, 2 front legs, and the loin in 3 pieces, separately reserving the blood and the liver. Place the hare in a large shallow nonreactive container with a cover. Combine 8 cloves garlic, the chopped onions, cubed carrots, bay
leaf, and parsley and thyme sprigs in a mixing bowl. Stir in the tannic red wine and
cognac along with 1 teaspoon of the pepper. Pour the mixture over the hare. Cover and
refrigerate for 7 days.

2   After 7 days, remove the hare from the marinade and pat dry. Place the hare in a shallow,
glass baking dish, cover with plastic film, and return to the refrigerator for an additional 24
hours. Transfer the marinade to a nonreactive container, cover, and refrigerate.

3   Preheat the oven to 350°F.

4   Heat the olive oil in a large sauté pan over medium-high heat. Remove the hare from
the refrigerator and place in the hot pan. Season with salt to taste. Sear, turning occasionally, for about 8 minutes or until golden brown on all sides. Using tongs, transfer
the hare to a platter.

5   Heat the duck fat in a large braising pan over medium heat. Add the diced onions and sweat for 5 minutes or until translucent, taking care that they do not brown. Stir in the tomato paste and then add the hare. Cook for 3 minutes. Blend in the flour and cook, stirring frequently, for an additional 8 minutes. Raise the heat and add the bottle of red wine. Using a wooden spoon, stir vigorously to deglaze the pan. Bring to a simmer; then lower the heat and simmer for 30 minutes or until the liquid is reduced by half.

6   Crush the remaining 5 cloves garlic and add to the pan along with the sliced carrot and ¼ of the reserved marinade. Again, bring to a simmer and simmer for 5 minutes. Add the Veal Jus and blanched pork rind and again bring to a simmer. Simmer for 8 minutes; then transfer to the preheated oven, cover, and braise for 1½ to 2 hours or until the meat is fork tender.

7   Remove from the oven and transfer the hare to a bowl. Cover with a clean, damp kitchen towel and keep warm.

8   Pass the sauce through a fine mesh sieve into a small saucepan, discarding the solids. Taste and, if necessary, adjust the seasoning with salt and pepper. Set aside.

9   Place the bacon in a medium sauté pan over medium heat and fry for 3½ minutes or until golden brown. Using a slotted spoon, transfer the bacon to a double layer of paper towels to drain.

10   Place the light olive oil in a medium sauté pan over medium heat. Add the pearl onions and sauté for 3 minutes or until just lightly colored. Season with salt to taste. Remove from the heat and keep warm.

11   Place the sauce over low heat to warm.

12   Place the liver and butter in a food processor fitted with the metal blade and process until smooth. Transfer the mixture to a small bowl and blend in the blood and Armagnac.

13   Remove the sauce from the heat and whisk in the liver-butter mixture. Pass the sauce through a fine mesh sieve into a clean saucepan. Place over low heat to just warm through.

14   Place the hare pieces on a serving platter. Scatter the bacon and pearl onions over the top and sprinkle with the cloves and parsley, and serve with the sauce on the side.

Venaison poilée, dans son jus

PAN-ROASTED VENISON WITH RASPBERRY SAUCE

parfumé à la framboise,

AND CABBAGE WITH PINK PEPPERCORNS

choux au poivre rose

● SERVES 4

I use Scottish roe deer for this dish because I particularly like its delicate flavor. However, if it is not available, the saddle of a farm-raised red deer will do just fine. Whichever you use, you must roast it with care as it must never be overcooked or the desired texture and flavor will be lost. It should always be served rare enough that, when sliced, the juices will run quite red and add the delicate yet gamy flavor to the fruity, acidic sauce. The short marination neither tenderizes the meat nor does it begin to cook it; using it only serves to enhance the naturally sweet flavor.

1 cup red wine, rich in tannins

½ cup raspberry vinegar

1 small Savoy cabbage, halved lengthwise, well washed and dried

8 juniper berries

½ cup plus 2 tablespoons unsalted butter

Coarse salt to taste

Freshly ground pepper to taste

2-pound saddle of Scottish roe deer or farm-raised red deer, trimmed and boned

3 tablespoons light olive oil

1 green bell pepper, well washed, halved, cored, seeded, white membrane removed, and julienned

1 red bell pepper, well washed, halved, cored, seeded, white membrane removed, and julienned

1 teaspoon pink peppercorns

Sel de Guerande to taste

1   Combine the red wine and vinegar in a small bowl. Cover and refrigerate.

2   Remove and discard the core from the cabbage. Cut the cabbage lengthwise into thin strips. Set aside.

3   Remove the marinade from the refrigerator and divide it into two equal portions. Place one portion in a small nonreactive saucepan over medium-low heat. Add the juniper berries and bring to a boil. Lower the heat and simmer for about 12 minutes or until the mixture is reduced by more than half and is slightly syrupy. Remove from the heat and beat in the butter, a bit at a time. Season with salt and pepper to taste and pass through a fine sieve into a bain-marie to keep warm.

4   Place the remaining marinade in a shallow dish large enough to hold the venison. Add the venison and marinate, turning occasionally, for 10 minutes.

5   Preheat the oven to 450°F.

6   Remove the loin from the marinade and pat dry with paper towels. Heat 1½ table-spoons of the olive oil in a medium ovenproof sauté pan over high heat. When it is smoking hot, add the loin and season with salt and pepper to taste. Sear, turning occasionally, for about 3 minutes or until the venison is nicely browned on all sides. Transfer to the preheated oven and roast for 5 minutes. Remove from the oven and allow to rest for 3 minutes.

7   While the venison is roasting, heat the remaining 1½ tablespoons of the olive oil in a large sauté pan over high heat. Add the cabbage and season with salt and pepper to taste. Sauté for about 4 minutes or until the cabbage has just begun to wilt slightly. Add the red and green bell peppers and sauté for an additional 2 minutes or just until the vegetables are al dente. Stir in the peppercorns and remove from the heat. Drain off any excess fat and spoon the vegetables into the center of a serving platter. Spoon the warm sauce around the edge.

8   Slice the loin crosswise into ½-inch-thick pieces and arrange the slices on top of the sauce. Sprinkle the meat with sel de Guerande and serve.

Selle d'agneau rôtie à

LAMB ROASTED ON THE BONE

l'os, crème l'estragon

WITH CREAM OF TARRAGON

● SERVES 4

Roasting any type of meat on the bone not only keeps it from drying out but also ensures that it will be juicy and succulent, holding all of its natural flavor. I believe that roasting on the bone even gives meat better texture. Using the meat's own fat for basting will also intensify the flavor. For a lamb saddle on the bone, it is best to use a prime butcher who is skilled at deboning quality meat. The flanks and ribs of the saddle should be removed and saved for use as a base for the roasting meat and as the main ingredient for the jus natural. The felt, the membrane on the fat cover, should be removed and discarded.

One 5-pound saddle of lamb, flanks, felt, and rib bones removed

Coarse salt to taste

Freshly ground pepper to taste

3 tablespoons light olive oil

2 tomatoes, well washed, cored, and cut into 2-inch pieces

1 onion, peeled and cut into ¼-inch dice

1 carrot, well washed, trimmed, and cut into ¼-inch dice

1 head garlic, well washed and cut in half, crosswise

1 bunch fresh thyme, well washed and tied in a bundle

½ cup white wine

1½ cups water

1 tablespoon plus optional 1½ teaspoons unsalted butter

2 bunches fresh tarragon, well washed and dried

6 shallots, peeled and cut crosswise into thin slices

1 clove garlic, peeled and crushed

2 tablespoons dried tarragon

2 cups Bouillon de Poule or White Veal Stock (see pages 282 and 285)

1½ cups heavy cream

1   Preheat the oven to 475°F.

2   Remove the lamb from the refrigerator and let sit at room temperature for 20 minutes.

3   Chop the flanks and rib bones into 3-inch pieces and set aside.

4   Season the flesh side of the lamb with salt and pepper to taste. Place in a large roasting pan and drizzle with 2 tablespoons of the olive oil. Place in the preheated oven and roast for 8 minutes.

5   Lower the temperature to 400°F. Remove the roasting pan from the oven and baste the lamb with its own fat. Lift the lamb saddle from the pan and place the chopped flanks and bones, along with the tomatoes, onion, carrot, head of garlic, and thyme, in the middle of the pan. Return the lamb to the pan, placing it on top of the bones and vegetables and return the pan to the 400°F oven, basting every 5 minutes. Roast the lamb for another 20 minutes. Lower the temperature to 325°F and continue to roast for an additional 20 minutes or until an instant-read thermometer registers 145°F when inserted into the thickest part.

6   Remove the roasting pan from the oven and transfer the meat to a serving platter. Tent lightly with aluminum foil to rest for 30 minutes and keep warm on the back of the stove.

7   Pour off all except 1 tablespoon of the fat from the roasting pan, keeping the trimmings, bones, and vegetables in the pan. Add ¼ cup of the wine and stir to deglaze the pan. Place over medium-high heat on top of the stove and bring to a boil. Lower the heat and simmer for about 5 minutes or until the wine has almost evaporated. Add the water and again bring to a simmer. Simmer, stirring occasionally, for about 10 minutes or until the liquid is reduced by one half. Taste and, if too salty, add 1½ teaspoons unsalted butter and a drop or two of water or, if too lightly seasoned, add salt and pep-

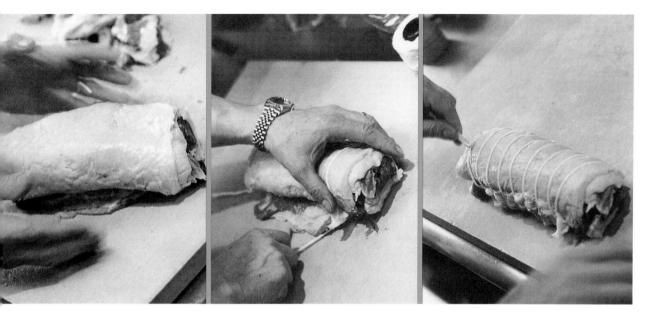

per to taste. Remove from the heat and strain through a fine mesh sieve into a clean container. Measure out ½ cup and set it aside. Refrigerate or freeze the remaining *jus natural* (natural sauce) in a tightly covered container for another use.

8 Remove the leaves from one bunch of the tarragon and set them aside. Chop the remaining stems along with the remaining bunch of tarragon and reserve them separately.

9 Bring a small saucepan of water to boil over high heat. Add the tarragon leaves and blanch for about 3 seconds or just long enough to set the color. Drain well and refresh under cold running water. Pat dry and set aside.

10 While the lamb is roasting, prepare the sauce. Heat the remaining 1 tablespoon each of butter and light olive oil in a medium saucepan over medium heat. Add the shallots and crushed garlic and cook for about 4 minutes or until just translucent. Stir in the dried tarragon and then deglaze the pan with the remaining ¼ cup of white wine. Cook for about 5 minutes or until the wine has almost completely evaporated. Add the bouillon and simmer for about 20 minutes or until reduced by half. Add the cream and the chopped tarragon and tarragon stems, and simmer for 20 minutes or until reduced by one half. Remove from the heat and place in a blender. Process to a smooth puree; then pass the sauce through a fine sieve into the top half of a double boiler over very hot

water. Add the reserved ½ cup natural lamb jus along with the blanched tarragon leaves. Taste and, if necessary, adjust the seasoning with salt and pepper to taste.

11 Using a sharp knife, remove the bone from the lamb saddle by cutting along the back bone and under the loin. You will now have two loins. Remove the two tenderloins, which are located just underneath the loins. Slice the loins, slightly on the bias, into thin pieces and arrange the slices down the center of a serving platter. Cut the tenderloins in half and place them along the side of the loins. Spoon the sauce around the meat and drizzle a bit over the top. Serve immediately.

Les Célébrités
New York City

In 1991, I was approached by Wolf Walter, the general manager of the Essex House Hotel in New York City (which was owned by Japan Airlines), to open a restaurant in the hotel. It was to feature *haute cuisine* and since I had been so successful at the Maurice, Mr. Walter felt that I could bring the coveted 4 stars to the star of the Nikko chain. I was to be chef for the restaurant—hands on and also supervisor of the restaurant Botanica, and banquets. The concept for the restaurant was the idea of Mr. Walter's wife; it centered on a collection of art works by celebrities that would be featured in the restaurant. From this came the obvious name of the restaurant, Les Célébrités, honoring the creators of the wall décor.

The idea intrigued me and I accepted the offer. Before I could begin work on the menu, however, I had to travel to Japan to meet the hotel's executives at their corporate headquarters as well as to work with chefs who would help familiarize me with the demands of the Japanese table. After Japan, I was also required to travel to Hong Kong and Taiwan. It was important to the executives that I should understand the needs, customs and cultures of these areas, as many of the hotel's clients would be representative of these lands. They also gave me the opportunity to travel to Italy and to spend two months with the esteemed chef Joel Robuchon at his restaurant, Jamin, in Paris. I traveled for almost one year while the restaurant was being built.

While traveling, I did many, many promotional dinners to introduce potential travelers to the Nikko Hotels as well as to lure them with the promise of fine dining at the premier hotel restaurant in New York City. By doing so, I got to work in many different restaurants in Japan and China, where I learned an amazing number of new (to me) cooking techniques as well as familiarizing myself with many of the ingredients that gave such distinct flavor to individual Asian dishes. Once, when I was preparing frogs' legs, I inquired as to their whereabouts. "Over there," I was told. I saw a fellow holding a couple of bags. When I approached him, he took the frogs, one at a time, from the bags and dispatched and cleaned them as I stood, mouth agape, right in front of him. This was truly as fresh as it gets!

I also got to shop some of the great markets of the world. In Tokyo, I spent many an early morning at the famous fish market watching unbelievably beautiful fish being ordered and prepared for sushi, sashimi, and other traditional Japanese dishes. I had never, and still to this day have not, seen anything as pristine as that market. In fact, throughout Japan, the markets are orderly and magnificently arranged. You can eat with your eyes as you shop—everything is so appetizing.

I finally returned to New York to prepare for the opening of Les Célébrités during the second week of October 1991. After seeing so much in my travels and immersing myself in the kitchen of Robuchon, it was now time to do my own thing. I had the years of training, my slow, steady climb up the kitchen ladder and my experience with Chef Senderens behind me. I determined that what I did would be recognized as my own individual style. I wanted to take the classics that I felt that I deeply understood and instill in them the fruits of my learning.

I had begun to move away from the heavy sauces of the classical repertoire. I wanted to incorporate the use of fresh fish that I had seen in Asia. I embraced the fruity olive oils of Italy. I wanted to stay with my heritage but introduce new and interesting products into it. The more that I thought about what I wanted to do, the more I realized that it was exactly what I had always done. Use the freshest locally grown ingredients, give them the respect they were due, and cook them in the simplest method possible that would serve to highlight their inherent goodness. The only real difference was that I could now get seasonal ingredients from all over the world within a day or two of their being picked, caught, or selected. And, after so many years in America and having an American family, I felt free to expand my culinary repertoire in a way that I probably never would have done had I stayed in France. So you can well imagine that it was with much excitement (and a fair amount of apprehension) that I took over the stove at Les Célébrités. The restaurant opened to a 3-star review in *The New York Times,* in which the menu was described as "a Zen-like harmony of East and West that is a joy to experience." My excitement and apprehension had worked together to help me push myself to broaden my understanding of fine dining. The whole staff, in the kitchen and in the front of the house, worked hard at creating an atmosphere of luxe. As a consequence, Les Célébrités became one of the few restaurants in the country to hold both the much-coveted Mobil five stars and the American Automobile Association's five diamonds.

The apogee of my career came in January of 1998 when I was awarded the *Medaille du Mérite Agricole* in recognition of my "outstanding accomplishments and contributions to French *haute cuisine* abroad." Only two medals have been awarded outside France each year since the medal's creation over one hundred years ago. The *Medaille du Mérite Agricole* honors food and wine professionals whose talents and achievements have supported the agricultural industry and its products. Former recipients of the *Medaille du Mérite Agricole* have included my colleagues Alain Sailhac and Jacques Pépin, the American journalist Jeffery Steingarten, New York City restaurateur Sirio Maccioni, and the founder of the French Culinary Institute in New York City, Dorothy Cann-Hamilton. What glorious company I keep!

Le Gazpacho de Crabe d'Alaska, Tomates Rouges et Jaunes
GAZPACHO OF RED AND YELLOW TOMATOES WITH ALASKAN CRAB

Tartare de Thon
TUNA TARTARE

Truite Fumée à la Minute
FRESH SMOKED TROUT

Burger de Foie Gras Pommes Vertes
FOIE GRAS BURGER WITH GRANNY SMITH APPLES

Oignon Farci
STUFFED ONION

Pomme à l'Ecrasée aux Truffes Blanches
WHITE TRUFFLE-CRUSHED POTATOES

Le Risotto de Homard et Truffes Noires
LOBSTER RISOTTO WITH BLACK TRUFFLES

La Chartreuse de Choux et Faisanne d'Ecosse
ROASTED PHEASANT WITH WINTER VEGETABLES

Le gazpacho de crabe

GAZPACHO OF RED AND YELLOW TOMATOES

d'Alaska, tomates

WITH ALASKAN CRAB

rouges et jaunes

● SERVES 4

This is the perfect soup for a hot summer's day when tomatoes are at their peak. Add a pungent, fruity olive oil and you have the full taste of Provence in a bowl. Alaska's king crab, with its sweet meat and briny overtones, is the quintessential complement to the fruity flavors. Processing the soup in a blender lets you choose the texture of the soup—smooth, slightly chunky, or very chunky, your choice! The Banyuls vinegar gives just an extra touch of sweet acidity to the soup.

2 ripe red tomatoes, well washed, cored, and quartered

½ large cucumber, peeled, seeded, and cut into 1-inch dice

½ Spanish onion, peeled and cut into 1-inch dice

¼ red bell pepper, well washed, cored, seeded, membrane removed, and cubed

½ cup extra-virgin olive oil

4 teaspoons Banyuls vinegar

Coarse salt to taste

Freshly ground pepper to taste

2 yellow tomatoes, well washed, cored, and quartered

¼ yellow bell pepper, well washed, cored, seeded, membrane removed, and cubed

5 ounces Alaskan crab leg meat, cut into ¼-inch dice

1   Place the red tomatoes along with half of the cucumber and onion in the bowl of a food processor fitted with the metal blade. Add the red bell pepper along with ¼ cup of the olive oil and 2 teaspoons of the vinegar. Process to a smooth puree. Season with salt and pepper to taste and process to just blend. Taste and, if necessary, add more olive oil and vinegar to balance the flavor. Push the gazpacho through a fine sieve into a nonreactive container. If the soup seems too thick, add a few tablespoons of cold water. Cover and refrigerate for 2 hours.

2   Using the yellow tomatoes and yellow bell pepper and the remaining cucumber, onion, olive oil, and vinegar, repeat Step 1.

3   When ready to serve, mound ¼ of the crabmeat into the center of each of four shallow soup bowls. (For a prettier presentation, use two soup spoons to shape the crabmeat into quenelles [see page 124]).

4   Remove the two soups from the refrigerator. Pour each soup into a pitcher. Take one pitcher in each hand and simultaneously pour the yellow and red soups into each soup bowl to create two half circles, one red and one yellow. Serve immediately.

Tartare de thon

TUNA TARTARE

● SERVES 4

When in Japan, I was impressed with the considerate approach to the handling of fish. The Japanese deeply respect their ingredients and are particularly adept at preparing fresh fish. In fact, they try to keep the fish as near to its natural state as possible, and when they do cook it, it is usually just passed through the heat. They never overpower the product but allow its natural goodness to shine. From the time I spent in Japan, I have tried to emulate this respect, so, very often, I barely cook the wonderful fish that is available to me.

I use only bluefin tuna, and when it is served raw, it has to be Japanese quality sashimi. This can be quite a challenge, even in New York City, but I have been lucky enough to find a supplier who regularly brings me the quality I seek. This is a very basic tartare recipe, which I will often garnish with round "petals" of gently roasted red, yellow, and green bell peppers for an exceptional presentation.

1½ pounds sashimi-quality bluefin tuna

3½ tablespoons extra-virgin olive oil

1 teaspoon soy sauce

Coarse salt to taste

Freshly ground pepper to taste

½ cup peeled and seeded tomato cut into ¼-inch dice

3 tablespoons minced fresh chives

1 teaspoon red wine vinegar

4 slices country bread, toasted, crusts removed, and cut into triangles

1   Using a sharp knife, remove the dark red blood part along the loin of the tuna. Cut the tuna into ¼-inch dice and transfer into a nonreactive container placed over ice cubes to keep the fish very cold. Add 3 tablespoons of the olive oil and the soy sauce and mix well. Season with salt and pepper to taste.

2   Combine the tomato, chives, and vinegar with the remaining olive oil in a small nonreactive bowl. Season with salt and pepper to taste.

3   Form the tartare into quenelles (see page 124) and place 2 quenelles in the center of each of four serving plates. Spoon the tomato mixture around the tartare and serve immediately with toast triangles.

Truite fumée à la minute

FRESH SMOKED TROUT

● | SERVES 4

This is the simplest method that I know of to create a lightly smoked delicate fish. Although it may seem a bit intimidating to put some wood chips in a frying pan to burn, it really does work and I've never had a fire in the kitchen doing it. The smoke is so faint and yet it does infuse the fish with a sweet, smoky flavor. There is just enough heat to set the flesh and keep it moist and delicious. The humble, and easy-to-make, potato salad offers just the right accent to make a perfect dish.

6 medium Yukon gold potatoes, cleaned and scrubbed

¼ cup extra-virgin olive oil

2 tablespoons minced shallots

1½ tablespoons fresh flat-leaf parsley julienne

1 tablespoon red wine vinegar

Coarse salt to taste

Freshly ground pepper to taste

3 to 4 tablespoons of hickory wood chips

4 boneless trout fillets, skin on

½ lemon, seeds removed

Fleur de sel to taste

I Place the potatoes in cold salted water to cover by at least 1 inch in a medium saucepan over medium-high heat. Bring to a boil and cook for 20 minutes or until tender when pierced with the point of a sharp knife. Drain well and allow to cool for 5 minutes.

2 While they are still warm, peel and cut the potatoes crosswise into ¼-inch-thick slices. Place in a bowl with 3 tablespoons of the olive oil and the shallots, parsley, and vinegar. Season with salt and pepper to taste. Gently toss to combine, taking care not to crumble the potatoes. Cover with a damp towel and keep warm.

3 Place a large heavy-duty frying pan on medium-high heat. Add the wood chips and heat for 4 minutes or until the chips start to burn. Splash a tablespoon of water over them to create more smoke. Place a wire rack (or grill) on top of the frying pan for 3 to 4 minutes or until hot.

4 Coat the fish with the remaining 1 tablespoon of olive oil and season with salt and pepper to taste. Place the fillets, flesh side down, on the hot rack (or grill) and cover with a lid. Cook for 3 minutes or until slightly firm. Turn off the heat and let rest, covered, for 1 to 2 minutes.

5 Uncover the pan. Peel off and discard the skin from the fillets.

6 Place an equal portion of the potato salad in the center of each of four plates. Place a fillet on top of the potatoes on each plate. Squeeze lemon juice over the trout and add a pinch of fleur de sel as a garnish. Serve immediately.

SERVING SUGGESTION To move this dish to new heights, I often garnish it with some crème fraîche and Osetra caviar. If the idea appeals to you, fold 2 to 3 tablespoons of Osetra caviar into 4 to 5 tablespoons of crème fraîche. Gently stir in a teaspoon of minced chives and a splash of lemon juice. Place a nice spoonful on top of the trout.

Burger de foie gras

FOIE GRAS BURGER WITH

pommes vertes

GRANNY SMITH APPLES

● SERVES 4

This version of foie gras with apples was, for many years, the landmark of my cuisine at Les Célébrités, with the apples taking on the role of the hamburger roll and the foie gras the burger. It was, for its time, the most exclusive burger in town. The full flavor and acidic taste of the Granny Smith apples serve to cut through the intensely rich fattiness of the foie gras. The apples also help to balance the unctuous flavor of the foie gras. It is a gorgeous dish full of color with a tiny bit of apple cider vinegar sauce as an accent. Perhaps it is a tip of my hat to my American father-in-law's gift at the cider press.

4 Granny Smith apples

½ tablespoon confectioners' sugar

2 tablespoons duck fat

2 tablespoons apple cider vinegar

½ cup Duck Jus (see page 287)

Four 3-ounce slices fresh foie gras

Coarse salt to taste

Freshly ground pepper to taste

1 tablespoon unsalted butter

1 Preheat the oven to 425°F.

2 Line a baking pan with parchment paper. Set aside.

3 Cut the apples in half crosswise. Using a paring knife, trim and round off the cut edges, hollow out the core, and reserve the trimmings. Place the confectioners' sugar in a small sieve and sprinkle over the cut side of each apple half.

4 Heat the duck fat in a sauté pan over medium-high heat until sizzling. Place the apples in the fat, cut side down. Reduce the heat to medium and cook for 5 minutes or until the apples are just tender and golden brown. Using a slotted spatula, remove the apples from the pan and place them on a double layer of paper towels to drain. Set aside.

5 Keeping the pan over the flame, reduce the heat to low. Add the apple trimmings and cover. Cook for 5 minutes or until the apple pieces are tender and all the juices have been released. Increase the heat to high and stir in the cider vinegar to deglaze the pan. Add the Duck Jus and simmer for 5 minutes or until reduced by half. Strain the liquid through a fine mesh sieve into small saucepan and set aside.

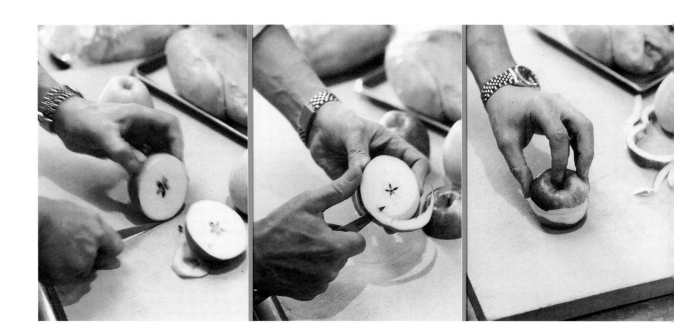

6   Season the foie gras on both sides with salt and pepper to taste. Heat a nonstick sauté pan over high heat until almost smoking. Add the foie gras and sear for 2 to 3 minutes on each side. Using a slotted spatula, remove the foie gras from the pan and place on a double layer of paper towels to drain. Set aside.

7   Place the apple bottoms, cut side up, on the prepared baking sheet; then place one slice of foie gras on top of each apple bottom. Place an apple top, cut side down, on top of the foie gras on each apple bottom to make "sandwiches." Place in the preheated oven for 2 minutes or until the apples and foie gras are warm to the touch. Remove the "sandwiches" from the oven and, using a slotted spatula, transfer them to a double layer of paper towels to drain.

8   Place the reserved sauce over medium heat and whisk in the butter until smooth. Season with salt and pepper to taste.

9   Using the spatula, place a "sandwich" in the center of each of four 3-inch plates. Spoon the sauce around the "burger" and serve.

1½ ounces fresh white truffle

Approximately 8 cups sea salt

4 large Idaho potatoes, well washed, dried, and pierced with a fork

1½ tablespoons white truffle butter

1 tablespoon unsalted butter

3 tablespoons white truffle oil

Coarse salt to taste

Freshly ground pepper to taste

Fleur de sel

1   Preheat the oven to 425°F.

2   Scrub the truffles with a small brush and a knife to remove any clinging dirt. (You can work them under running water, but they must be dried very well immediately or they will quickly get spongy. You can also store them for 2 to 4 days in a tightly covered glass container filled with Arborio rice to absorb any moisture.)

3   Make a 1-inch layer of sea salt in a large baking dish. Nestle the potatoes into the salt and place the dish in the preheated oven. Bake for 1 hour or until the center is tender when pierced with the end of a small, sharp knife. Remove from the oven and lift the potatoes from the salt.

4   Cut the potatoes in half lengthwise. Using a spoon, remove the flesh and place it in a shallow mixing bowl. Discard the skins.

5   Using a fork, lightly crush the potatoes. Add the truffle butter and unsalted butter and continue to crush until almost smooth. Add the truffle oil and continue to crush until well blended. Season with salt and pepper to taste. Spoon an equal portion of potato in the center of each of four serving plates. Using a truffle slicer, slice an equal portion of truffle over the top on each plate and sprinkle with fleur de sel. Serve immediately.

Le risotto de homard et

LOBSTER RISOTTO WITH

truffes noires

BLACK TRUFFLES

● SERVE 4

In this recipe no one ingredient is dominant; each one has a role to play in the partnership. When the inexpensive, everyday rice is cooked to perfection it is very creamy, almost unctuous, with a bit of crunchiness. It becomes the supporting equal to the lobster and truffle, luxe ingredients at the high end of the food chain. It is important that the lobster be as creamy as the rice, which the poaching in Beurre Blanc helps ensure, and that the truffle comes in at the end to add a jolt of earthiness and a final boost to the entire dish.

2 tablespoons olive oil

1 small onion, peeled and cut into ⅛-inch dice

8 ounces Arborio rice

¾ cup dry white wine

6 tablespoons unsalted butter

Two 1¼-pound lobsters

1½ cups warm Beurre Blanc (see page 290)

3¼ cups Bouillon de Poule (see page 282)

2½ tablespoons skimmed milk

2½ tablespoons black truffle oil

¼ cup freshly grated Parmesan cheese

3 tablespoons black truffle butter

Coarse salt to taste

Freshly ground white pepper to taste

2 ounces fresh black truffle, cleaned

1   Heat the olive oil in a medium saucepan over medium heat. Add the onion and sauté for about 3 minutes or just until translucent. Add the rice and sauté for an additional 2 minutes. Add the wine and simmer for 5 minutes or until the liquid has been absorbed. Remove from the heat and allow to cool to room temperature.

2   Cut 2 tablespoons of the butter into ½-inch dice and place in freezer. Reserve the remaining butter at room temperature.

3   Place the lobsters in a large pot of boiling salted water. Poach for 4 minutes. Immediately, drain well and shock in an ice-water bath. When they are cool enough to handle, remove the shells. Chop the claw meat into ¼-inch dice and cut the tails lengthwise into 2 pieces.

4   Combine the lobster tail pieces with warm Beurre Blanc in the top half of a double boiler placed over hot water to keep warm.

5   Return the rice to medium heat. Add 2½ cups of the bouillon and bring to a simmer. Simmer for about 7 minutes or until the rice is al dente and most of the liquid has been absorbed.

6   While the rice is cooking, prepare the foam base. Place the remaining ¾ cup bouillon in a small saucepan over medium heat and bring to a simmer. Add the skimmed milk, followed by 1¼ tablespoon of the truffle oil. Reserve in warm plate.

7   Stir the cheese into the rice. Remove from heat and stir in the truffle butter and the remaining 1 tablespoon unsalted butter. Season with salt and pepper to taste and continue stirring for 1 to 2 minutes. Add the reserved chopped lobster claw meat along with the remaining truffle oil.

8   Spoon an equal portion of the risotto into four shallow soup bowls. Using an immersion blender, whip the reserved foam base, blending in the frozen butter cubes as you whip. Spoon the foam around the risotto. Place a piece of the lobster tail meat in the center of the risotto on each plate and, using a truffle shaver, shave truffles over the top. Serve immediately.

La chartreuse de choux

ROASTED PHEASANT WITH

et faisanne d'Ecosse

WINTER VEGETABLES

● SERVES 4

I really love the quality of Scottish pheasant. I have even had the opportunity of visiting the hunting grounds of Scotland with my friends Georges Faisan and Arianne Daguin, owners of D'Artagnan, the specialty meat purveyors. It was an extraordinary experience that I remember every time I roast one of these magnificent birds. I only use the breast meat of female pheasant because I find it to be much more delicate in flavor. The only problem is that it cannot take the slightest amount of overcooking. I have devised the method in this recipe that I think will insure a perfectly cooked bird. Finished "à la minute"—that is, just before serving—in the rich foie gras fat, the meat remains moist and succulent.

2 Scottish female pheasants, washed and patted dry

Coarse salt to taste

Freshly ground pepper to taste

2 tablespoons unsalted butter

6 cups Bouillon de Poule (see page 282)

2 tablespoons unsalted butter

4 large leaves Savoy cabbage, trimmed

2 turnips, peeled and trimmed

lenge, as they had, for quite some time, concentrated on Gray Kunz's demanding yet freewheeling examination of exotic seasonings and Asian flavors and techniques. Classical French cooking as they understood it seemed boring and old hat. Once we got in sync and the crew, both back and front, appreciated the importance of the fundamentals as they related to my desire to lighten, simplify, and explore the elemental repertoire, the juices ran.

Two months after arriving at Lespinasse, my dream was realized. Ruth Reichl, the esteemed restaurant reviewer for *The New York Times*, awarded us the coveted 4 stars, saying in her review opening, "If the dining room at Lespinasse were a person, it would be smiling today. After a long marriage with a chef determined to put the décor in the shadows, it has finally found a compatible partner." This was just what I had hoped to achieve when I first set foot in the kitchen. I wanted to create a menu that would be equal to the extravagance of the dining room but, at the same time, would not be intimidating to the diners. I am ever grateful to the amazing staff that came together to insure that my dream came true.

From the beginning, however, the restaurant has been accused of charging exorbitant prices. So much so that *The New Yorker* magazine even wrote a rather humorous op-ed piece on the $35 price of my Soupe de Poireaux et Pommes de Terre Langoustines et Truffes Blanches.

However, to meet the demands of a 4-star rating, it is necessary to buy only the best, and the best costs a lot! Truffles, which I use extensively, can range up to $2,000 a pound, langoustines often reach $20 per pound, beluga caviar may reach almost $3,000 a kilo, and on and on. Even simple vegetables like carrots, potatoes, and leeks, when grown organically by a small farmer, can cost four to five times more than their supermarket cousins. So, when all is said and done, the restaurant may just break even on the $35 soup! And, for the diner, I hope that my search for perfection is worth the extravagance of the moment!

As long as I am facing critics, I should also state that, along with the high prices associated with my menu, I have, I know, often been called an old-fashioned, demanding French chef. I would like to think that my attitude in the kitchen, much like my menu, has mellowed over the years. I do know that keeping to my principles has exacted a toll and has, from time to time, made for a strained atmosphere in the kitchen. However, I do believe that my passion for what I do has never wavered and that I have, over the years, passed it on to many young chefs. It is this, after all, that is the most important aspect of what I do. Unless I can teach others to continue the legacy of classical cooking, my time in the kitchen will have been wasted.

I have been working in kitchens for over forty years. From the beginning, I only wanted to do the best job that I could. I was, after all, trained as a technician, not as a creative artist. The creativity is something that evolved over the years and, I believe, only blossomed as I immersed myself in the freedom and experimentation allowed by my adopted American culture. I remain very much a French chef. It would be impossible for me to move away from the home cooking that I learned from my mother and grandmothers or the techniques and methods that I absorbed in my early years in classic French kitchens. However, I like to think that as I expanded my own understanding of the rules covering the chemistry of culinary creation, I have been able to master the simplicity of creating a perfect meal. *Bon Appétit!*

Soupe de Courge 'Butternut,' Magret et Foie Gras de Canard,
Feuilles de Choux de Bruxelles

BUTTERNUT SQUASH SOUP WITH DUCK BREAST, FOIE GRAS, AND BRUSSELS SPROUT LEAVES

Soupe de Poireaux et Pommes de Terre, Langoustines, et Truffes Blanches

POTATO LEEK SOUP WITH WHITE TRUFFLES AND LANGOUSTINES

Ragoût de Légumes Miniatures Mijotés á l'Huile d'Olive, Truffes et Sel Gris

RAGOUT OF BABY VEGETABLES WITH BLACK TRUFFLES, OLIVE OIL, AND GRAY SALT

Foie Gras Sauté aux Pêches Blanches et Sauternes

SAUTÉED FOIE GRAS WITH WHITE PEACHES

Grosses Coquilles St. Jacques, Emulsion Légère au Curry, Feuillantines
aux Graines de Sésame

SCALLOPS WITH CURRY SAUCE AND SESAME TUILES

Saumon Confit à l'Huile d'Olive, Petite Salade de Roquettes, Vinaigre Balsamique

SALMON CONFIT IN OLIVE OIL WITH ARUGULA SALAD AND BALSAMIC VINEGAR

Homard Poché en Coque, son Bouillon Réduit à l'Estragon, Carottes à l'Écrassées

MAINE LOBSTER POACHED IN THE SHELL WITH TARRAGON-SCENTED BOUILLON
AND CRUSHED CARROTS

Langoustines Poêlées, Truffes, Mousseline de Choux-Fleurs

LANGOUSTINES WITH CAULIFLOWER AND BLACK TRUFFLE MOUSSELINE

Sole Farcie d'une Mousse de Saint Jacques Truffée

DOVER SOLE WITH TRUFFLED SCALLOP MOUSSE

Filet de Bar à la Vapeur, Sauce Vierge, Salade de Haricots Verts au Caviar Osetra

STEAMED BASS WITH A SALAD OF FRENCH GREEN BEANS AND OSETRA CAVIAR

Poularde Farcie, Truffes, Pochée dans Son Bouillon

STUFFED CHICKEN WITH TRUFFLES POACHED IN BOUILLON

Canette de Barbarie Rôtie à la Broche, Compote de Cerises Acidulées

ROASTED MUSCOVY DUCK WITH CHERRIES

Cochon de Lait Confit

CONFIT OF BABY PIG

Côte de Veau Pochée et Rôtie, Mousseline d'Artichauts, Artichauts Farcis

POACHED AND ROASTED RACK OF VEAL WITH STUFFED ARTICHOKES AND
ARTICHOKE MOUSSELINE AND NATURAL SAUCES

Selle et Carré d'Agneau, Epaule Braisée et Couscous

RACK AND LOIN OF LAMB WITH BRAISED LAMB SHOULDER AND COUSCOUS

Soupe de courge "butternut,"

magret et foie gras de canard,

feuilles de choux de bruxelles

● SERVES 4

This is really nothing more than a great garbure with only one vegetable as its base. The recipe for the basic soup reflects my desire to separate the richness and fatty mouth feel of the garnish with a true, clean, and uncompromising essence of the squash. The duck and Brussels sprout garnish also moves the soup from homespun to restaurant luxe. Some sautéed chicken or, in fact, any meat could substitute for the duck, since the squash is so mellow, that it will pair with almost anything. Although the soup could be made with a more traditional chicken stock and provide excellent results, this more contemporary method that uses water accentuates nature's sweet and noble squash flavor.

¼ cup duck fat

5 ounces slab bacon, cubed and blanched

1 medium onion, peeled and cut into ¼-inch dice

3 cloves garlic, peeled

3 medium butternut squash, peeled, halved, seeded, and cubed

Coarse salt to taste

8 cups water

½ pound Brussels sprouts, cored, leaves pulled apart, well washed, and dried

2 ounces chanterelle mushrooms, cleaned and trimmed of any dry parts

1 pinch fines herbes

Freshly ground pepper to taste

1 single boneless Moulard duck breast, skin on

4 ounces fresh duck foie gras, from the small lobe if possible

2 tablespoons unsalted butter

1. Melt 2 tablespoons of the duck fat in a large, deep Dutch oven over medium-high heat. Add the bacon and the onion, and sweat them for about 5 minutes or until the onions are translucent and the bacon has just begun to cook. Do not allow either one to take on any color. Stir in the garlic and sauté for a minute. Add the butternut squash and season with salt to taste. Add the 8 cups of water and bring to a boil. Simmer for 25 minutes or until the squash is very tender. Strain through a fine sieve, straining the liquid into a clean saucepan. Set the solids aside.

2. Place the cooking liquid over medium heat and bring to a simmer. Lower the heat and slowly reduce the liquid for 10 minutes to set the squash flavor.

3. Transfer the reserved squash mixture to a blender. With the motor running, slowly add the reduced liquid, processing to a smooth puree. Taste and, if necessary, adjust the seasoning with salt to taste. Pour the puree into the top half of a double boiler placed over simmering water to keep warm. Alternately, cover and refrigerate until ready to use for up to 2 days and reheat when ready to serve.

4. Bring salted water to boil in a 2-quart saucepan over high heat. When boiling, add the Brussels sprout leaves and blanch for 1 minute. Using a slotted spoon, drain the leaves and shock them in ice water. Place the leaves on a double layer of paper towels to drain; then transfer to a small plate. Set aside.

5. Heat 1 tablespoon of the duck fat in a sauté pan over medium-high heat. Add the chanterelles and the pinch of Fines Herbes and sauté for 5 minutes or just until the mushrooms have begun to color slightly. Season with salt and pepper to taste. Using a slotted spoon, lift the mushrooms to a plate and tent lightly with aluminum foil to keep warm.

6. Using a sharp knife, score the fatty skin side of the duck breast without cutting into the meat. Heat a heavy-bottomed skillet over high heat. When very hot but not smoking, add the duck breasts, skin side down. Season with salt and pepper to taste and sear for

5 minutes or until nicely browned and crisp. Turn the breast and continue to cook for an additional 6 minutes or until the meat is medium-rare and slightly firm to the touch and the exterior is nicely browned. Transfer the duck to a plate and tent lightly with aluminum foil to keep warm.

7   Pour the fat from the skillet and return the skillet to high heat. Add the foie gras. Sear for 1 minute per side. Using a slotted spatula, lift the foie gras to a double layer of paper towels to drain. Immediately transfer to a plate and tent lightly with aluminum foil to keep warm.

8   Heat the remaining tablespoon of duck fat in a medium sauté pan over medium heat. Add the reserved Brussels sprout leaves and sauté for about 2 minutes or just until the leaves start to take on some color.

9   Lift off the top half of the double boiler and place it over high heat. Bring the soup to a gentle boil and whisk in the butter. Taste and, if necessary, adjust the seasoning with salt and pepper to taste.

10 Place an equal portion of the chanterelles in the center of each of four shallow soup bowls. Using a sharp knife, cut the duck breast, on the bias, into thin slices. Place 2 slices on top of the chanterelles in each bowl. Cut the foie gras, on the bias, into four slices and place one on top of the duck in each bowl. Ladle an equal portion of the soup into each bowl and serve.

Soupe de poireaux et pommes

POTATO LEEK SOUP WITH WHITE TRUFFLES

de terre, langoustines, et

AND LANGOUSTINES

truffes blanches

● SERVES 4

After all these years, I am still tinkering with the classic Potage Parmentier that I learned in hotel school so many kitchens ago. The master recipe is, of course, the same that you will find on page 72, but I think that this is the most luxurious example yet. The base is such a perfect example of the excellence of fine French cooking that I felt it could be taken to new heights with the addition of the magnificent langoustines and truffles. The simplicity of the soup only accentuates the voluptuous nature of the shellfish and truffle.

3 tablespoons unsalted butter

1 medium onion, peeled and chopped

6 medium leeks, white part only, well washed and chopped

Coarse salt to taste

2 cups Bouillon de Poule (see page 282)

1½ cups water

1½ Idaho potatoes, peeled and cut into 1-inch dice

1 cup leek julienne, white part only

2 cups Beurre Blanc (see page 290)

4 langoustines, shelled and cleaned

1 tablespoon crème fraîche

Freshly ground pepper to taste

4 teaspoons white truffle oil

1 golf-ball-size white truffle, well cleaned

1. Heat 2 tablespoons of the butter in a medium saucepan over medium-high heat. Add the onion and sauté about 4 minutes or until the onion has sweat its moisture but has not taken on any color. Stir in the leeks and continue to cook for an additional 5 minutes. Season with salt to taste and cover. Bring to a simmer; then lower the heat and simmer for about 10 minutes or until all of the moisture has been extracted from the vegetables. Increase the temperature to medium-high and add the bouillon and water. Bring to a boil; then lower the heat and simmer 10 minutes. Add the potatoes and again bring to a simmer. Simmer for about 15 minutes or until the potatoes are tender when pierced with the point of a small sharp knife. Remove from the heat.

2. Place the potato mixture along with any liquid in a blender and process to a smooth puree. Strain through a fine mesh sieve into the top half of a double boiler. Taste and, if necessary, season with additional salt. Place the top half of the double boiler over simmering water to keep the soup warm. Do not cover.

3. Melt the remaining 1 tablespoon butter in a small sauté pan over medium heat. Add the leek julienne and sauté for about 3 minutes or until al dente but without any color. Set aside and keep warm.

4. Place the Beurre Blanc in a shallow saucepan large enough to hold the langoustines in a single layer. Add the langoustines and place over medium heat. Bring to a bare simmer; then lower the heat and cook for about 3 minutes or just until the meat is beginning to firm. Remove from the heat.

5. Remove the top half of the double boiler and place it over medium-high heat. Bring the soup to a boil. Immediately remove from the heat and whisk in the crème fraîche and remaining butter. Season with salt and pepper to taste.

6. Place an equal mound of leek julienne in the center of each of 4 shallow soup bowls. Place a langoustine on top of the leeks and drizzle white truffle oil over the leeks. Using a truffle grater, shave the truffle over the top. Ladle the soup into the bowls and serve immediately.

Ragoût de légumes

RAGOUT OF BABY VEGETABLES WITH

miniatures mijotés à l'huile

BLACK TRUFFLES, OLIVE OIL, AND GRAY SALT

d'olive, truffes, et sel gris

● | SERVES 4

This recipe can only be made at the height of the growing season when the baby vegetables are absolutely at their finest. They must be dew-drop fresh and preferably organic with all the goodness of the earth in every bite. If you choose to make this in the winter, use only tiny, organically grown root vegetables along with, perhaps, some baby bok choy or other baby winter greens. The truffles and fruity oil only serve to acknowledge the earthiness of the dish and the sel de Guerande balances the flavors to perfection.

8 long baby carrots, peeled and trimmed

8 round baby carrots, peeled and trimmed

8 baby turnips, peeled and trimmed

8 radishes, well washed and trimmed

4 stalks baby white asparagus, well washed and trimmed

4 haricots verts or green beans, well washed and trimmed

¼ cup fresh fava beans, tough outer skin removed

¼ cup fresh English peas

1 tablespoon olive oil

8 chanterelles, brushed clean and trimmed of any dry parts

Coarse salt to taste

3 cups light Bouillon de Poule (see page 282)

4 teaspoons chopped black truffles

1 teaspoon diced shallots

1 teaspoon minced chives

8 red or yellow olive or currant tomatoes

¼ cup lemon-scented olive oil

Sel de Guerande

4 sprigs fresh chervil

4 sprigs fresh tarragon

1   Make a large bowl of ice water. Set aside.

2   Bring a large saucepan of salted water to boil over medium-high heat.

3   Working with one type of vegetable at a time, blanch the carrots and turnips for 6 minutes, the radishes for 5 minutes, the asparagus and haricots verts for about 2 minutes, and the fava beans and English peas for 1 minute, or until each vegetable is al dente. Immediately shock each vegetable in the prepared ice-water bath to stop the cooking.

4   Heat the olive oil in a small sauté pan over medium heat. Add the chanterelles and sauté for about 3 minutes or just until warmed through. Season with salt to taste and remove from the heat.

5   Place the bouillon in a large shallow braising pan over medium-high heat. Add the reserved carrots, turnips, radishes, asparagus, haricots verts, fava beans, and English peas, and cook for about 2 minutes or just until warm. Remove from the heat and pass through a fine mesh sieve, separately reserving the vegetables and the bouillon.

6   Carefully transfer the vegetables to a shallow bowl. Add 2 tablespoons of the reserved bouillon along with the truffles, shallots and chives. Gently mix, taking care not to break the vegetables.

7   Place an equal portion of the vegetables in 4 shallow soup bowls. Add an equal portion of the tomatoes, reserved chanterelles, and lemon-scented oil to each serving, along with a pinch of sel gris. Garnish each plate with sprigs of chervil and tarragon, and serve.

Foie gras sauté aux pêches

SAUTÉED FOIE GRAS WITH WHITE PEACHES

blanches et sauternes

I almost always combine foie gras with some kind of fruit. In midsummer, it is peaches, preferably white ones, that make the association. Although they have an indescribably refined flavor with just a hint of acid, peaches are also quite meaty in texture. I find this tanginess and density to be a perfect foil for the silken liver. In the Rhone valley of France, late summer offers the "Pêche de Vignes," a peach that is actually almost wine red inside with a very acidic tang, which is an even better match for foie gras. If it were available in New York, it would be my first choice for this dish. I'm only telling you this so that if you ever find this French peach, you will know what to do to turn it into a taste of heaven on earth.

½ cup water

½ cup plus 1½ tablespoons sugar

½ cup dry white wine

4 cups Sauternes wine

4 white peaches, well washed and dried

2½ tablespoons unsalted butter

½ cup fresh raspberries, well washed

Four 2-ounce, 1½-inch-thick slices fresh foie gras

Coarse salt to taste

1　Combine the water with ½ cup of the sugar in a medium nonreactive saucepan over high heat. Bring to a boil; then lower the heat and simmer for 10 minutes. Add the white wine and again bring to a simmer. Add the Sauternes and simmer for an additional 30 minutes or until the liquid is syrup-like. Remove from the heat and set aside.

2　While the syrup is simmering, prepare the peaches. Cut the peaches in half lengthwise. Remove and discard the pits and trim around the edges to make each peach half round, smooth, and all of the same size. Add the peach trimmings to the simmering wine mixture.

3　Gently place the peaches in the simmering wine mixture and bring to a boil. Lower the heat and poach for 2 minutes or until the skin starts to peel away from the flesh. Using a slotted spoon, transfer the peaches to a plate and allow to rest until cool enough to handle. When cool, using your fingers, slip the skin from the peaches. Add the skins to the simmering syrup.

4　Continue to simmer the wine mixture for about 45 minutes or until it is the consistency of a very thick syrup. (It is the perfect consistency when a teaspoonful spooned onto a cold plate does not run, but stays together in a puddle.) Strain the syrup through a fine mesh sieve into a clean bowl, discarding the solids. Set aside and keep warm.

5　Preheat the oven to 400°F.

6　Heat 2 tablespoons of the butter and the remaining 1½ tablespoons of sugar in a medium nonstick sauté pan over medium heat. Add the peaches, cut side down, and cook, turning occasionally, for 10 minutes or until golden and nicely caramelized. Using a slotted spatula, transfer the peaches to a warm plate and keep warm.

7　Return the sauté pan to medium heat. Add the remaining ½ tablespoon of butter along with the raspberries. Gently crush the berries with a fork to make a chunky puree and cook, stirring frequently, for 2 minutes. Remove from the heat, set aside, and keep warm.

8　Season the foie gras on both sides with salt to taste.

9　Heat an ovenproof nonstick sauté pan over high heat until almost smoking. Add the foie gras and sear for 30 seconds on each side. Transfer to the preheated oven and cook for another 2 minutes. Using a slotted spatula, remove foie gras from the pan and pat dry both sides with a paper towel.

10　Place a peach half, cut side up, in the center of each of four 9-inch plates. Place a spoonful of the raspberry sauce in each peach hollow. Place a slice of foie gras on top of each peach. Top with a remaining peach half, cut side down. Drizzle the Sauternes syrup on the top of each peach and around the edge of the plate, and serve immediately.

Grosses coquilles St. Jacques

SCALLOPS WITH

émulsion légère au curry,

CURRY SAUCE AND

feuillantines aux graines de sésame

SESAME CRISPS

● SERVES 4

For some years now, I have been getting divers' sea scallops from New England and Nova Scotia. The quality and freshness is unbelievable. They are so sweet, you can eat them like candy! If you are not so lucky, just make sure that you purchase scallops from a reputable fishmonger. They must not be packed in brine since, to keep their integrity intact, they must be quite dry when cooked. In the restaurant kitchen we say, "Sear a scallop on one side and kiss it on the other." The spicy curry complements the sweet scallops beautifully, the tomatoes add a flavor-enhancing note of acidity, and the Feuillantines add a nice finishing crunch.

12 jumbo sea scallops, muscle removed and patted dry

¾ pound fresh spinach

3 tablespoons olive oil

¼ cup minced onion

3 tablespoons curry powder

Cochon de lait confit
PAGE 266

*Selle et carré
d'agneau, épaule
braisée et couscous*
PAGE 274

Sole farcie d'une mousse de Saint Jacques truffée   PAGE 256

Concassé de tomate

TOMATO CONCASSE

1½ tablespoons unsalted butter

2 tablespoons minced shallots

3 ripe tomatoes, peeled, cored, seeded, and finely diced

Coarse salt to taste

Heat the butter in a medium sauté pan over medium heat. Add the shallots and sauté for about 4 minutes or until just soft and translucent. Add the tomatoes and season with salt to taste. Cook, stirring occasionally, for about 12 minutes or until the liquid has reduced by half. Remove from the heat and keep warm until ready to serve. (Alternately, place in a nonreactive container, cover, and refrigerate until about 30 minutes before ready to use. Remove from the refrigerator and let come to room temperature.)

Saumon confit à l'huile d'olive,

SALMON CONFIT IN OLIVE OIL

petite salade de roquettes,

WITH ARUGULA SALAD AND

vinaigre de balsamique

BALSAMIC VINEGAR

● SERVES 4

The idea to confit salmon is not original to me but one gleaned from kitchen gossip where recipes and experiments from chefs all over the world are discussed. I learned that many chefs were slowly cooking fish in duck fat but I thought that since salmon is so fatty to begin with, it would be better served if it was slowly cooked in something other than animal fat. Copper River salmon is my first choice for this dish but if it isn't available look for Alaska salmon. Both of them are very fatty and the fat really does make a difference as it ensures a very smooth texture in the finished dish.

4 cups light olive oil

Bouquet Garni (see page 293)

Four 6-ounce boneless, skinless Copper River salmon filets

1½ pounds micro arugula, washed and patted dry

Sel de Guerande to taste

4 teaspoons aged balsamic vinegar (see note)

Bouillon de poule

CHICKEN STOCK

Two 6- to 8-pound stewing hens, well rinsed

4 medium onions, with skin, cut in half crosswise

9 tomatoes, washed, cored, and cut in half crosswise

4 leeks, white part with some green, well washed

4 carrots, washed and trimmed

2 heads garlic, excess skin pulled off and cut in half crosswise

2 Bouquet Garni (see page 293)

1 tablespoon peppercorns

1   Place one hen in a large saucepan at least three times its size with cold salted water to cover by at least 1 inch (this should be at least 1 gallon of water). Place over medium-high heat and bring to a simmer. Lower the heat and simmer gently for 10 minutes, frequently skimming off the fat and impurities that rise to the surface.

2   While the hen is simmering, place 4 onion halves, cut side down, on a stovetop grill or in a cast-iron skillet over medium heat. Grill, turning occasionally, for about 10 minutes or until the onions have blackened. This will give the bouillon a golden color.

3   Add the grilled onions to the bouillon along with 4½ tomatoes, 2 leeks, 2 carrots, garlic, 1 Bouquet Garni, and half of the peppercorns. Raise the heat and again bring to a simmer. Lower the heat and gently simmer for 3 hours or until the meat is falling off the bone and the bouillon is a deep golden color. It is important to maintain the same water level throughout the entire cooking period, so it is necessary to add cold water. The addition of cold water will momentarily stop the simmering and will allow all of the impurities to rise to the surface. Skim the surface well and frequently during cooking, as this will ensure the clarity of the bouillon. Remove from the heat and strain the bouillon through a fine mesh sieve into a clean container placed in an ice-water bath. Discard the solids. Skim off any remaining fat and impurities from the surface of the bouillon as it cools.

4   Begin the cooking process again following the above procedure without blackening the onions. Add the remaining hen, vegetables, Bouquet Garni, and peppercorns. Add the bouillon from the first cooking along with enough water to cover by 1 inch. Season

Fresh breadcrumbs

To make breadcrumbs to be used in stuffings: Trim the crusts from fresh, standard American white bread. Cut the bread into quarters and place in a food processor fitted with the metal blade. Process, using quick on and off turns, to a medium-fine crumb. Do not dry the bread or the crumbs.

To make breadcrumbs to be scattered on top of a dish to be baked or *gratinéed*: Trim the crusts from French bread. Cut the bread into thin slices and place on a baking sheet to dry for at least 6 hours. Place the dried bread in a food processor fitted with the metal blade. Process, using quick on and off turns, to a fine crumb.

Cutting a stencil

1   Stencils may be cut from cardboard or from firm pieces of thin plastic. For the latter, plastic lids or tubs make a good resource. Cardboard stencils will be good for only one use; plastic can become a permanent kitchen utensil. Stencils can be cut into any shape that you desire. However, they are usually no more than 10 inches long and 3 inches wide. They are traditionally used in the pastry kitchen to make *tuiles*, thin, crisp French cookies that are often cooled over a rounded form to make a curved shape resembling a roof tile (*tuile*).

2   Stencils are laid directly onto a nonstick baking sheet and, with a pastry brush or flexible spatula, the batter is spread over the stencil and carefully lifted up so that a perfect shape is left on the baking sheet.

Index

Tart(s):
    Apple, Upside-down, 156–157
    Mom's Apple, 56–57
Tartare de Thon, 208–209
Tarte:
    aux Pommes Bonne Maman, 56–57
    Tatin, 156–157
Terroir, 215
Thyme, Scallop Raviolis with Zucchini and, 170–171
Tomato(es):
    Concasse, 245
    Confit, 292
    Gazpacho of Red and Yellow, with Alaskan Crab,
        206–207
    Rabbit Stew with Mushrooms and, 142–143
    Sauce, with Scallops, Curry Sauce and Sesame
        Crisps, 242–244
Tourner (cutting technique), 30
Triple Bouillon de Poule, 284
Triple Chicken Stock, 284
Troika (Montreal), 161
Trout:
    with Almonds and Cream, 84–85
    Fresh Smoked, 210–211
Truffle(s):
    Basmati Rice, Truffled, 296
    Black
        Cauliflower Mousseline and, 255
        Langoustines with Cauliflower Mousseline and,
           252–254
        Lobster Risotto with, 220–221
        Ragout of Baby Vegetables with Olive Oil,
           Gray Salt and, 237–238
    cost of, 229
    Poached in Bouillon, with Stuffed Chicken, 260–262
    Ravioli, Celery and, 172–173
    White
        Leek and Potato Soup with Langoustines and,
           235–236
        Potatoes, White Truffle-Crushed, 218–219
Truite:
    aux Amandes les Charmilles, 84–85
    Fumée à la Minute, 210–211
Tuna:
    bluefin, 208
    Tartare, 208–209

U

Upside-down Apple Tart, 156–157

V

Vanilla:
    Cream Custards, 98–99
    Ice Cream, with Armagnac Prunes, 100–101

Veal:
    jus, 286–287
    Poached and Roasted Rack of, with Stuffed
        Artichokes and Artichoke Mousseline and
        Natural Sauce, 268–269
    selecting, 268
    Stew, 94–96
    Stock, White Veal, 285
Vegetables. *See also* names of vegetables
    blanching, 8
    Chicken in a Pot with Stuffing and, 34–36
    Cooked in White Wine and Herbs, 177–178
    Ragout of Baby Vegetables with Black Truffles,
        Olive Oil, and Gray Salt, 237–238
    Roasted Squab with Pea Sauce and, 189–190
    Spring, with Lamb Stew, 91–93
    stewing, 80
    Winter, with Roasted Pheasant, 222–223, 225
Vegetable Soup in the Gascon Style, 22–23
Venaison Pôilée, dans son Jus Parfumé à la
        Framboise, Choux au Poivre Rose, 194–195
Venison:
    Pan-Roasted, with Raspberry Sauce and Cabbage
        with Pink Peppercorns, 194–195
    Roasted, with Grand Veneur Sauce, 144–145
Vinegar, Balsamic, *see* Balsamic Vinegar

W

Walter, Wolf, 202
Waste, eliminating, 6
White Peaches, Sautéed Foie Gras with, 240–241
White roux, 94
White Truffles:
    Leek and Potato Soup with Langoustines and,
        235–236
    Potatoes, White Truffle-Crushed, 218–219
White Veal Stock, 285
White Wine:
    Artichokes with Herbs and, 29–31
    in Roasted Venison with Grand Veneur Sauce,
        144–145
    sauce, 82–83
    in Sautéed Foie Gras with White Peaches, 240–241
    Vegetables Cooked in Herbs and, 177–178
Wild Boar Stew, 148–150
Windows on the World (New York, NY), 167
Wine, 2. *See also* Red Wine; White Wine
Winter Vegetables, Roasted Pheasant with, 222–223,
    225
Women, as best French chefs, 2
Wonton skin wrappers (for raviolis), 170

Z

Zucchini, Scallop Raviolis with Thyme and, 170–171